# Healing Begins With The Mind

(Solutions for the New Millennium)

Youssef Khalim

Copyright © 2013 Youssef Khalim
All rights reserved.
ISBN: 978-0-9787798-6-3
ISBN-13: 978-0978779863

# DEDICATION

To: Larisa Khalim (The real or ideal soul mate: inspiration).

Tonya Tracy Khalim and

Runako Soyini Khalim, (my most beloved daughters).

Mother and Grandmother and Great-grandmother, (my most beloved maternal biological ancestors, and spiritual antecedents).

M. A. Garvey (one of my 7 M's: my role models).

Youssef Khalim II; III (my most beloved sons).

Father and Grandfather and Great-grandfather, (my most beloved paternal biological ancestors, and spiritual antecedents).

To: The Forerunners and Reincarnation sources (beloved biological ancestors and spiritual antecedents), and

The Almighty (our Spiritual Father), from whence we come.

# CONTENTS

|     | Acknowledgments | i |
| --- | --- | --- |
| 1 | Introduction | 1 |
| 2 | About the Observation Reports | Pg 3 |
| 3 | What's On Your Mind? | Pg 4 |
| 4 | Observations of Noah | Pg 7 |
| 5 | Observations of Susan | Pg 17 |
| 6 | Observations of the Author | Pg 21 |
| 7 | Healthy Psychological Inventories | Pg 28 |
| 8 | The Myers-Briggs Type Indicator | Pg 35 |
| 9 | Do Dreams Reflect Any Reality? | Pg 37 |
| 10 | Introduction to Dreams and Visions | Pg 39 |
| 11 | The Dreams and Visions | Pg 41 |
| 12 | How's Your Energy Level? | Pg 46 |
| 13 | Update: Observations of Noah | Pg 61 |
| 14 | My Delightful Sun | Pg 62 |
| 15 | Noah is Great | Pg 63 |
| 16 | Prayer-I | Pg 64 |
| 17 | Update: Observations of the Author | Pg 65 |
| 18 | Update: Observations of Susan | Pg 69 |
| 19 | Barack Obama to Complete the Presidency of Abraham Lincoln | Pg 70 |
| 20 | The Solution to Our Economic and Social Future: Jubilee and Other Remedies | Pg 75 |
| 21 | Index | Pg 96 |
| 22 | About the Author, and Other Books | Pg 105 |

# ACKNOWLEDGMENTS

To: The Forerunners and Reincarnation sources (beloved biological ancestors and spiritual antecedents), and

The Almighty (our Spiritual Father), from whence we come.

# 1 INTRODUCTION

In *Healing Begins With The Mind*, Khalim considers psychological/psychiatric questions and concerns, and presents possible solutions. He finds the fields of psychology/psychiatry, themselves, to be substantially dysfunctional; overly negative, morbid, hypocritical, irresponsible, oppressive, racist, corrupt, dishonest, ignorant of necessary fundamental information, misguided, overly intrusive, and subsequently ineffective.

He says a healthy mind should know the first reality- a higher force in the universe, which we refer to as God. Khalim feels that the field is further handicapped by operating in, and trying to conform to an irrational and evil economic system and social order. Therefore, these very practitioners become predators against the people that they are supposed to serve. He believes that too many people in the field do not have sufficient morality, values, or character requirements to try to minister to people's minds.

He is uneasy about an area and function (mind) which should have high respect and even reverence, being intruded into by base, corrupt, immoral, and oft-times anti-God people who are trying to make a living for themselves, or even abuse others. And he believes that the practitioners here have assumed a function which was previously the province of spiritually advanced shamen or priests. He believes that anyone in the field should have high morality and correct values.

Khalim asks, "Why is it that the general historical, pervasive sickness and hypocrisy of society, the West, and the U.S.A. (in particular) has not been recognized and addressed?" He advocates testing everyone to determine personality characteristics like introversion-extroversion, thinking-feeling, and intuition-perceiving tendencies. People should know whether they have left, right, or whole brain dominance. And people should know their overall adjustment (or maladjustment) level.

He believes this can help identify a Mozart, Hitler, George Washington Carver, Daniel Hale Williams, Stevie Wonder, Gwendolyn Brooks, Martin Luther King Jr., Michael Jordan, liars, thieves, oppressors, materialists, the selfish, cowards, crooks, and people who are called devils.

He says that a system which he calls a test of the Energy Functionality of individuals can be used with a (possibly) reformed psychology/

psychiatry to help identify personality characteristics, tendencies, strengths, and weaknesses. He feels that a combination of tools can be used to help insure that people who probably will (and generally) do abuse authority and people are identified and monitored so that abuse does not take place. Conversely, potential benefactors of humanity can be identified.

He asserts that materialists, oppressors, and deviants really have low self-esteem because they have rejected (or do not know) who and what they really are. Then they try to make themselves into somebody by collecting things, getting control, power (or jurisdiction) over others. Then they abuse others, or their positions because they really do not have morality. And because of the laws of nature, they get caught up in their own vicious cycle- becoming more and more deformed and dysfunctional.

He believes people should know their biological lineage to help give a sense of belonging and linkage to the family, community, the planet earth, and ultimately, the universe.

# 2 ABOUT THE OBSERVATION REPORTS

There are three (3) Observation Reports included, and they are nonstandard. They include 1). The one-day observations of a toddler who will be 16 months old on 7-17-95. There is the possibility of his being gifted because both his parents were determined to be likewise. Also, two specific dreams indicate that possibility. (See dream numbers 5 and 12). Dream #12 shows him with a hat, or headband on; and that is an ornament, or adornment of the head. Number 5 is very specific, but it is not absolutely certain that it refers to him (or that whoever said he would be gifted is correct).

Observation #2 is of the mother of the child. And she has developed an emotional disorder. There is a description of the condition, and what may be done to treat it.

Observation #3 is of the father of the child, and it contains descriptions of the father using quotations from the MMPI (Minnesota Multiphasic Personality Inventory), the Myers-Briggs Type Indicator, and the Brain Dominance theories. There is also a list of the 17 dreams (two were mentioned above) of the youngster. The father had the dreams. There are various suggestions that may be applicable and useful to a greater understanding, rehabilitation, and appreciation of exceptional children.

*Healing Begins With The Mind* says, "God is the first reality, and this is the first thing that the aspiring healthy mind can learn. And in God, all things (including us) move and have their being. To be healthy one should eat plenty of fruits and vegetables, exercise, drink lots of water, get fresh air, think right, speak correctly, and take right actions. And when souls really want to become healthy again, they find their way back to the open arms of God."

# 3 WHAT'S ON YOUR MIND?

Well the subject of healing is on your mind. But, first, what is mind? How does it function? How can we take inventory of it? What is a balanced mind? How can we improve the mind? What is a sick mind? Who are those with sick minds? What are the consequences of a sick mind? How can you tell whether a mind is, on balance, healthy or sick?

How can a sick mind be healed?

In psychological terms, how do we view the mind, and its various conditions? What are the other ways that we may view the mind?

What are some examples of wholesome, healthy, and optimum minds?

And what about certain states of mind? What is the dream state? What is the conscious state?

What are visions? What are the senses? What are headaches?

Now, you and I know the mind is a very active fellow. It wants to know: What is laughter? What is having a sense of humor? What is sexuality? What is homosexuality? What is truth, beauty, knowledge? What is Babel? Babylon the Great? What is nationalism?

What is religion? IQ? What is intelligence? Memory? Carbon 14 dating? What are virtues? What is love, anger, hate, fear, courage, impotence, death, heaven, hell, sin, guilt, blasphemy, sacrilege, the devil?

Did Jesus and the early Christians heal with such awesome results? What, or who is Christ? What is the Messiah? Who was Moses, Muhammad? If the body is the temple of the Living God, is He centered in a specific location? Can God really communicate with us? If so, how? Does God punish? Does God really care about human life? Is there a judgment? If so, when?

What is prayer? What good is it, if any? Is there such a thing as "miracles?" Where did the body of man come from? Is the human body the product of a kind of Darwinian evolution? How old is mankind? Why do we have different "races" of mankind?

Were there other settlements of mankind on earth during the time of "Adam?" If so, where did they settle, and when? How can we increase the vitality, or longevity of man?

We cannot answer any of the above questions without first looking at the big picture. In the overall scheme, we are mind, body, and soul. When these aspects work in harmony and balance within one individual, and he retains vigor, energy, and a positive impact on his surroundings, and worthwhile pursuits in life, then he is healthy.

Soul is higher spirit, and that part of the God-Force which exists in higher evolution. Therefore, it has been said that God created man in His image. And man has free will accompanied by enormous potential (for both good, and evil). And so, soul is highly evolved spirit. And we just think of ourselves as sparks of God, manifesting in suitable places throughout the universe, for growth and development.

When the soul reaches a certain level of maturity, and it understands that all creation is One, and that God is Love, and sharing; and it reaches a balanced understanding of the physical plane, and the spiritual plane, (and it demonstrates an understanding of these), it graduates, and returns to God.

"Well, what about this active fellow called mind," you say. "Where did it come from?"

We say, "Soul produces mind." And we further say, "Soul has been involved in producing everything," including the body. But, in a way, we say (speaking more precisely), the mind produces the body, for it is that force which (most directly) has to live there. And the evolution of the body can be worked on from without." Go back and look at the Gospel, according to John.

And so, it is important to remember that the body evolved much like Darwin has said, but there are important links missing in his data."

"Aha," you say, "So, we've been co-producers with our Father, all along?"

"Well, I think you've got it, by Jove," I say.

"But what's this stuff about God?," you say. "You're mixing in the subjects of mind, body, soul, God, (and everything else under the sun). "How does this relate to the topic here, which is supposed to be about the mind?"

We say, "God is the first reality. And He does exist. Mind is a process by which we subdivide God into time , space (and the various objects in time and space) so that on a conscious level, we may understand Him."

"Now, what are you talking about?," you say. "Are you saying that time and space are not real?

"Not really," I say. "I'm saying, all things are relative. Don't go to work tomorrow two hours late, and then tell your supervisor that you're not really late because time is not really real."

"Could you move on," you say.

"No problem," I say. "Cause time's a-wasting." And the subject of God does boggle the mind, even if we divide Him into time and space (and the objects therein) - to make Him 'real.' Just look on the earth. Look in the skies! He never, never, ever ends. God never, never, ever ends. And God is real! And God is real! The Lord our God is real!"

So, God is the first reality, and this is the first thing that the aspiring healthy mind can learn. And in God, all things (including us) move and have their being.

Once upon a time, there was this guy named Renee' Descartes, who is reputed to have said, "I think, therefore I exist." And some people have considered him to be pretty smart. But if he had really been smart, he would have concluded, "I think, therefore God exists." For, again, we move and have our being (life) in Him!

One of the next things a healthy mind can learn (on an intellectual, and experiential level) is that we live in a causation world. And nothing is exempt from the law. As you sow, so will you reap. "Every step you take, every move you make, every thought you think, every eye you wink," comes under the same law. And some laws (like gravity) can be compensated for, so that flight is possible. And God can override some laws with the Law of Grace. The lesson here is that it is in one's own self-interest to treat others like we want to be treated because everything that happens has been predetermined by the will, actions, or inactions of individuals, or various forces. And you will have the goodness, or the negativity (that you do) returned to you!

And we know that the state of mind is something that can be altered or affected with the appropriate stimulus, or resources. And we will focus on the mind. And we will bring a Revolutionary Force of Goodness into the mind. And we will will the Power of God through soul, and through our mind and body! And this is an Unstoppable Force. For, it is the Force of God!

# 4 OBSERVATIONS OF NOAH

On June 24, 1995, the following observations of Noah were noted:

1. Description of Subject:

Noah is a 15-month-old toddler, as of 6-17-95. His weight and height were noted to be about 2 months ahead of his chronological age when he was about 6 months old. He weighed 10-pounds, 6 ounces at birth. Currently, he is about 30.5 inches tall and weighs about 24.5 pounds.

His walking became sufficiently proficient during the time he was 9-10 months old. So, we date his "walking" from that time. He has at least 11 teeth, including 3 molars. He says some words, like key, pop, "valk" (for walk), ball, mama, car, et.al. It is not clear to the observer how one would spell his pronunciation of "dog."

2. The observations took place at or near the residential setting of 1000 Blackhawk Drive, University Park, and in Park Forest, Illinois.

3. The observations were made Saturday, 6-25-95, beginning at about 3:30 P.M. Noah was picked up by automobile in Park Forest, just north of University Park, Illinois. He greeted the observer by extending his arms to be picked up. After being picked up, he gave a customary, long hug. At times he likes to cuddle. After getting the supplies needed to sustain him, we were shortly in the car.

It is usually very difficult to get Noah to ride in his car seat. He almost always wants me to hold him in the customary hug posture described above.

But, first, he wanted to play with the steering wheel, the gear stick, and the door lock. After a few minutes, I was able to get him somewhat under control. We drove to Jewel Food Store, in Park Forest.

We got out of the car. I carried Noah toward the Jewel food store as he looked all around. The wind was blowing strongly against his face. So, I tried to shield him partly from that by pulling his face against my chest.

In the store, he reached out for the grocery cart as we approached it. I put him in the seat, and we were off. Meanwhile, Noah is looking all around at the people, and at the products as we move past the checkout counters and the service counter.

I maintain an ongoing conversation with Noah as we move toward the Produce Department:

"How you doing Noah? Good to see you. I really missed you. What have you been doing? Have you been doing OK? Are you being treated OK? I'm so glad to see you. I love you, Noah. Soon, I'll be able to see you all the time." Soon we reach the Produce Department.

"Would you like some nectarines?"

Noah says, "pears." Or, so it seems.

"Nectarines, Noah. I'm going to see if we can't get you some pears too. Nectarines!" "Let's find you some soft pears, Noah." We select the pears, and three apples. And I repeat the names to Noah as we select:

"Apples, Noah. Pears." We move on and get some bread.
"We have to get some bread, Noah. We need some bread for the raccoons, too." We get two loaves of bread.
We get some other items, and we get some apple juice so Noah will have something to drink. We get pretzels. He likes them a lot.
"We're getting some pretzels for you, Noah. You want some pretzels? You want some chips, too?" The pretzels are put into the cart. Then, Noah decides that he wants to hold them. He only holds them for a few minutes.
He indicates that he wants to eat them, but I tell him, "Wait, Noah. We're going to have some later."
A few isles later, Noah indicates that he wants to be carried. I take him from the cart, and he gives me a big hug. I gently pat him on his back. Noah cuddles.
"Good to see you, Noah. Good to see you." I kiss him on the cheek. He seems so cuddly, so warm. So fragile. He seems so dependent.
"I love you Noah. I love you."
We get some lemon-lime pop. Noah loves pop. "You want some pop?"

"Pop!" He says. "Pop!"

"Pop, for Baby Cakes," I say. Sometimes, I call Noah "Baby Cakes," but I usually call him "Noah."

When we get to the Dairy Section, Noah indicates that he wants to ride in the cart again.
At the checkout counter, Noah reaches out and touches some items as they are

put on the conveyor. The names are repeated for him: "Pears, Noah. Nectarines. ice cream, mouth wash...."

Noah indicates that he wants to be picked up. I pick him up and he immediately reaches and touches the gum, on his left.

"It's gum, Noah. Gum."

Then, behind me, another customer smiles at Noah.

"Hi!" She says. "Hi there!" Noah holds on to me more tightly. He looks at his admirer, but he says nothing. He pretends to be shy. He clings to my chest, and eyes the woman.

We are now facing the cashier. She speaks to Noah, but he just looks at her. He extends his right hand slightly, and she put an orange sticker on it.

"Hello, handsome," she says. "Hello, cutie."

Noah says something as he tries to peel the sticker from his hand. I help him peel the sticker off as we move toward the exit.

The groceries are loaded into the cart. Noah is put into the seat. And we move out toward the car.

"We're going home now, Noah."

"Car," says Noah.

"Yes, we're going home in your car." Noah reaches for me to take him out of the grocery cart as we reach the car. He touches the car.

"Car, Noah." I pick Noah up and take him back over to the cart parking area. We

then go over and get into the car. I encounter the same problems as mentioned

before in trying to get Noah into his car seat. Then we're off to University Park.

Music is turned on. Immediately, Noah begins to move to the music. Back and

forth he goes. And we move down Western Avenue, through the forested area.

"You see the trees, Noah? Trees." The music is turned off. Noah begins talking again.

Finally, we reach our destination and Noah is allowed to pretend to drive the car a few minutes.

After we exit the car, Noah stands as I remove the groceries. He leads the way to the front door. We go inside.

Before I can finish putting the groceries up, Noah wants to go back outside.

"Valk!" He says.

"Noah, don't you want some pretzels first?" I open the pretzels and give him two. He puts one in his mouth and holds one in his hand. We go outside. He runs down the walkway, across the grass, going north. He runs, then walks down the sidewalk. Then, he sees a water pipe, terminated at about grass level. And he wants to examine it.

"Water pipe, Noah. Water pipe." Then, he tries to say what I have said. And we move on. The stem of a dandelion catches his eye. He breaks off about half. He then breaks off just about all of the remaining part, leaving only the base.

"Dandelion, Noah. Dandelion." And we "valk" some more, moving north. At about this time, Noah is watching two men, talking, and standing beside a car.

As we get closer to them he wants me to pick him up. And he listens to them. He turns his head to watch them as we pass.

"How's it going?" I say.

"How you doing?" They respond.

After moving about 25 feet north of the men, Noah again wants to walk. He lets me know by trying to get down, and verbalizing.

About this time, Noah hears and sees some children, across the street. He starts out into the street. He wants to get over to where they are. I try to hold his hand as we cross. But he snatches away. I try again. He refuses to cooperate. I then pick him up and carry him across the street. When I put him down, he starts moving toward the children, watching and listening.

When we arrive parallel to them, Noah first tries to follow one of the female youngsters who is about his size. He then tries to follow a boy, probably of school age. He is talking, but the boy just smiles at Noah because he can't understand him.

"Say, 'Hi!' Noah. Say, 'Hi,'" This continues a few minutes, and then we move north. And Noah indicates that he wants to be picked up.

As we move into the schoolyard where he likes to play, Noah indicates that he wants to get down and walk. Immediately, he begins to pick up rocks in the schoolyard driveway.

"Rocks, Noah. Rocks. No! Don't put that in your mouth!"

Noah now throws one of the remaining rocks. And we move to the area where he likes to play. That area has two bike rails parallel to each other and about 12 feet apart. Noah runs over to one rail and pulls himself up. He put his feet on the bottom tubing of the rail. And then he laughs and smiles about his accomplishment. Then, he goes over to the other rail and repeats the process. Two times he stopped and did the routine involving rocks.

I helped Noah navigate across one pipe that he must cross to get to the main rail. He gave me a hug a few times, the famous Noah Hug.

After about 40 minutes, we headed south, and repeated much of our experience while heading north. However, there is some difference. There is a dog across the street from the schoolyard that barks at us. Noah vigorously waves his arm at the dog. If there is hostility in the dog's barking, it does not register with Noah.

We move south, on the east side of the street. We pass a tree. Noah reaches for a branch.

I jump up, toward the tree limb. Noah thinks this is funny. I jump. He laughs. Noah

breaks off a twig.

"Tree, Noah. Leaves. Leaves, Noah. Those are leaves." Noah breaks off leaves, about one or two at a time. And he throws them in the air, and smiles, and makes sounds to show his pleasure. We head back south. And occasionally, I jump in the air (at Noah's urging), to make him laugh. Back at the house, he drinks some juice.

"Pop," he says. "Pop." Then, he heads for the back door. And he says his word for dog, because we have raccoons that come for bread at the back door. He seems to think that the raccoons are dogs.

I give the raccoon some slices of bread. Noah touches his hand to the glass door. And he talks to the raccoon.

"Raccoon, Noah. Raccoon. It's your raccoon."

Noah finally leaves the back door and gets some more juice. He then goes into the living room. He sees his 2.5 inch, orange, rubber ball.

"Ball," he says. He throws it. I catch it. "Ball."

When I give the ball back to him, I say, "Thank you." Noah gives me a hug, but it is a brief hug. His breathing is heavier than normal. He heads for the door.

"Valk," he says. Noah gets out the door and walks hurriedly down the walkway. When he reaches the drive way, he throws the ball. We repeat the ball routine. He thinks this is real funny.

Then, Noah heads across the grass, going north. He reaches some bricks, and he stops. He puts the ball into the opening in the bricks. I take it out. He puts the ball into the bricks.

When I give him the ball, I say, "Thank you."

Now, Noah wants to walk some more. But instead of allowing him to go north, as before, I pick him up and cross the street. And we go south, toward the library. We meet a lady with a small dog. Noah struggles to get to the dog. He calls to it.

"He likes children," the lady says. He won't bite. Noah puts his finger on the dog's face. He tries to get closer to put his hand on the dog's head.

"You like the dog, Noah? You like the dog?" After a few minutes, I almost drag Noah away from the lady and the dog. The lady moves on. We move on, south. In front of the library parking lot, there is a partially enclosed Bus Stop and benches. Noah likes to throw his ball over the bench, against the wall, so that it comes back to him or me, either over or under the bench. He throws it. I get it. (You know the routine by now).

He thinks this is fun. He stops at times and gives me a hug. He walks through the grass. I pick him up and we go over to the west end of the library parking lot and watch the fields below. It seems that Noah may be getting a little tired. He is still and quiet as I hold him in my arms.

"We're going back now, Noah. Are you ready to go home?"
We approach my neighbor's house. They have stairs. Noah twists. He tries to get down to go and climb the stars. I put him down and he runs toward the stairs. So we climb the stairs. I hold his arms, and he climbs the stairs, one at a time. Up we go! And down we go, twice. Then, I drag Noah away.

We stop at the tree in front of my home where Noah collects another twig. We enter. He gets some more juice, and he eats some applesauce, cereal, and bread. He seems to get a second wind.

First, he plays with his sister, Runako. She is lying on the sofa, face down. Noah puts his face to hers and gives her a kiss.

I say, "Man, he hasn't given me a kiss in a long time!"

She tries to play with him more, but he heads for the typewriter. And he hits on the keys. Then he goes over to the right end of the piano, and he hits some keys. He continues this, moving to the lower notes.

Then, I say to him, "Noah, what you doing?" I play with him for a few minutes. Then, he sees his orange ball. He plays with the ball, and a car that he can ride on. He opens the trunk and puts the ball inside. He tries to reach his hand through the opening to get the ball. He decides that the opening is too small, and that he must open the trunk to get the ball.

Noah holds up the car with one hand and spins a wheel with the other. Spin, spin, it goes. Then, he lets the car back down.

The air conditioner is on and air is blowing from the vent in the floor. Noah puts his hand on the vent to feel the air flow. After a few minutes, he stands above the air vent, legs spread apart, playing with the air.

Then he plays with the metal, spring doorstop, on the wall. He bends the spring and then lets go. He does this a few times.

"Noah, don't play with that. Let's go wash your hands." I take him into the washroom. And he eagerly reaches into the face bowl. Splash! Splash, he goes, stirring in the water. He tries to get a toothbrush. He gets the top of a pen. I get him out of there and dry his hands.

In the bedroom, he notices the phone, and he wants to talk on it. I call one his uncles:

"Hello! How's it going there? Noah wants to talk on the phone, so I thought you two might 'holler' at each other."

"Well, put him on."

"Say something, Noah. Say something."

"Hey!" Said Noah.

"Say something more, Noah. Tell him something else." Noah pushes the phone away.

"Well, Fred, I guess he doesn't want to say much more."

"Well, he did say, 'Hey!'"

"Ok, I'll talk to you later." I hang up the phone. And I take Noah into the living room.

"Book," he says. He reaches for the Encyclopedias. He takes down volume #6 as I hold him and get him into a good position. He repeats the word, several times:

"Book!"

"Your books, Noah," I tell him, because they were purchased especially for him. He takes down four of the books. And we put them on the cocktail table. Then, he starts turning the pages, from front to back. And then he turns from back to front. And I tell him what many of the pictures, or illustrations are about.

Then, he sees the flashlight on the bookshelf. And he reaches for it. I take it down, and shine it in his face, moving the light left and right.

He laughs and reaches for the flashlight. He shines it in his face, and he smiles. He plays with it a short while. He looks over toward the door.

"Valk," he says.

It was soon about 8:00 o'clock, and I wanted Noah to be slowing down. I like to put him to sleep before taking him back to Park Forest. I prepare to put him in his sleepwear. And this is sure to be the understatement of the year: "It is usually not easy to change Noah's pamper and put him into his sleepwear."

I take off his shoes first, and pretend that I'm going to bite his feet. I nibble at his feet, and growl. He just loves it. He laughs. And he kicks. And he laughs. Finally, I get him changed. He quickly gets down off the bed, and heads for the living room, and the front door.

"Valk," he says. But he stops in the washroom. He spins the roll of toilet paper. Spin! Spin, it goes.

I pick him up. "Noah, come on."

I hold him in my arms, outside the house. It is getting cooler now. Comfortable. Noah cuddles wonderfully. He is truly slowing down. I bring him inside, and I note that it's almost time to be taking him north. I lie down, with Noah on my chest. And I try to do our relaxation and healing exercise. I go through the exercise quickly. It's just about time to go, and Noah did not go to sleep today-yet. Sometimes he goes to sleep during the 12 minute drive north. When we arrive, Noah is cuddling. I try to get him to go to his care taker. After a few minutes, he goes to her for a few seconds, then he reaches for me. I take him again and he cuddles while I gently pat his back. I try to give him to her, and he threatens to cry. I hate to leave him. He hates to see me go. Finally, we try distracting him so that I can sneak out before he cries.

In conclusion, Noah needs to be around some virtuous people who really love him. These people must possess intelligence, and demonstrate sharing and caring attributes. They must have an awareness of our Creator, and of our mission to serve Him first- and then to be of service to mankind.

He should not. He will not- spend too much time with selfish, materialistic types infected with the dominant culture of this society.

First, he will be taught that he is a Muslim. He will be taught that just like Moses, Aaron, Joshua, Malcolm, Martin, King David, King Solomon, the Pharaohs, the Hebrews, et.al., his paternal roots are African. And he will be taught that he is one of the Sons of God.

Noah seems to have little or no fear of dogs, cats, or raccoons. He must be monitored closely around animals, until he learns to be cautious and circumspect. All necessary precautions must be taken for his safety.

He does seem to show some concern about being around strangers. This is a positive, if it is not taken too far.

He is really attracted to children. The concern here is that, in time, he learns to share. And he will learn that he cannot always get his way.

It will be a fact that Noah will be very much catered to. That is a result of various circumstances, and probably will continue. Obviously, I cannot spend all of the time with Noah that he would want, or that I would want. He especially needs some females in his life that fit the description of virtue, above.

As much as possible, he should be around people who are healthy in mind, body, and soul. He can be expected to be very strong-willed, and very loving, almost as part of his DNA. And we already see much of that.

His energy level is very high. And it must be channeled and guided carefully. He will need a certain freedom, but it is very important that he be taught proper constraints. He will be taught his full heritage.

In fact, I have set out much of what Noah will be taught in a book dedicated to him and entitled, "The Resurrection of Noah."

Noah has a wonderful laugh- and smile. Everyone will want to make him laugh. But when he cries, as someone else has observed, it is too deep and sorrowful. He seems to say, "Why are you doing this to me?" And I, for one, really don't want to hear him cry.

Many of Noah's prospects are very good. Both of his parents were viewed as "gifted" in their formative years. Both were Honors Students in High School.

His father has been called very talented. And that same designation goes back at least two generations in his paternal lineage. His father is also in touch with him on many levels. (See some of the experiences, attached).

Noah has been roundly blessed. And so, he may continue to be a focus and center of attention. Part of the good feeling about seeing Noah, and being with Noah is the realization that the world simply HAS TO IMPROVE TO BE A PLACE WORTHY OF HAVING NOAH.

As for the caregiver, we nominate her (and my mother) for Mother of The Year, for 1994 and 1995.

# 5 OBSERVATIONS OF SUSAN

(Observations made at various times)

1. Description: Susan (this is not her actual name), is the mother of Noah.
2. The observations took place at or in the vicinity of University Park, and Park Forest, Illinois.
3. The observations took place at various times.

## Background

As mentioned in the observations of Noah, (concerning his parentage), his mother was recognized as being "gifted" in her formative years. Reportedly, she excelled in mathematics and science.

When she was about 13, she had an accident in a gymnastics class, and she received an injury similar to what the actor Christopher Reeves recently experienced. She was in "traction" for a while. The spine (back), and/or the head sustained injury. She did recover, and as mentioned earlier, she was an Honors Student some time during High School. But sometime in her later teens, there were indications of maladjustment. And there are also indications of possible genetic predisposition to disorder.

## Observations

One observation really stands out. On about May 16, 1993, Susan engaged in a conversation about the role of men and women in marriage, or in a relationship. And she spoke with absolute confidence, clarity, knowledge, and wisdom. She spoke in a slight British, or Australian accent. She was articulate. She was eloquent. And I was really awe struck. I felt that I was in the presence of someone with very high intelligence.

I had never before, nor have I since observed her with that demeanor, or presence. Before that time I had observed her in various stages. Some seemed normal. Some seemed disordered. None indicated that she was highly intelligent. One impression about that time was that she was possibly a spoiled brat.

I have talked to Susan about that occasion many times. I used to feel that if we could dig this temperament and awareness out of her, and keep it at the conscious level, then we could fix the problem that exists here. She has even written a number of responses to my bringing up that matter. Basically, she has said that she does not have multiple personalities. In fact, she consistently denies that she has any problem whatsoever.

-Here I will give an important observation:

*All disease, or dysfunction is a result of imbalance, or the lack of integration within the organism. Or, it is a result of a lack of balance and harmony with its environment.* I still feel that we should have the opportunity (if Susan is willing) to use a method where we try to unify the mind! Unify the body. Unify the soul, and unify these aspects with each other. And then unify with Unity, (The Creator). And then, to allow the healing energies to flow through the individual. And this could be a partial or total solution to the problem. For, to date, the current methods are a dismal failure! And they've been tried for many, many years. The reason they don't work is that the practitioners don't know what they're doing. And they have an incomplete and distorted understanding of human beings.

They have been so busy studying rats and lower animals, and *trying to remake man in that image, that they have really missed the boat.*

Man's true nature is that of an individualized, unified energy field, or force. We call it soul, or spirit. It is a spark of what we usually call God. This soul, or spirit then exists within the flesh (along with another tool which it uses, called mind). This force must be kept unified within itself (of mind, body and soul), and remain unified with God to be healthy. *Man has creativity and imagination - and with that (and God), he can do just about anything* (given the time). Rats and lower animals don't have that capability.

Also, the materialist psychologists, and their fellow travelers don't understand dreams, visions, time, space, God, etc. And then a lot of them are liars and manipulators. A lot of them are busy trying to make a job for themselves, because of the irrational economic system that they live under. So, it is no wonder they have very limited success.

Anyway, that is a kind of side issue. I have come to know by experience that the problems existing here with Susan are very serious disturbances, and they cover the full range of what we know as mental dysfunction.

The symptoms cover the milder forms of neuroses, the psychopathic personality, and the psychoses. They're all there. So, I will not list them here. It would be easier to say what is not there.

So, what are the prospects? And what should be done?

-An observation is that she can act quite normal. However, when she comes under stress, dissociation quickly develops, (she quickly falls apart).

-How can we call up that really composed and intelligent individual that I mentioned earlier. And what is that all about?

-She feels that her father can, and will fix any problem for her, and provide her with what she needs or wants. And she feels that he will do whatever it takes-to do what she wants. And there is no sense of what is right, or what is wrong.

-It has also been observed that her father asks not whether she is being truthful, but he lets her manipulate him to do her bidding. He has said, "She really pulled herself together," (in referring to an instance where she was engaged in wanton lying about substantive matters) to the possible detriment of others. And again, there is no sense of what is right, and what is wrong.

-There also seems to be a propensity by her, and maybe another person close to her to rely on chemicals, medicines, etc., instead of trying to get the body to do natural healing- and to attain natural balance.

-She will say that she wants to be independent, but then she makes herself almost totally dependent- on her father. And she has a lot of fear and apprehension about displeasing him.

-One positive factor is that she can be very loving. She can be kind, considerate, and affectionate.

But what are the prospects for Susan? It really depends on her. If she doesn't Have a conscience, and knows what is right and wrong, and acts accordingly, then the problem becomes more difficult. It must also be remembered that some people are secure and comfortable where they are in life. And they do not really want to change into a better person.

It is important (for good mental health), for all of us to know on an intellectual, and on an experiential level that we are *all* children of God - all of us.
-It is important for us to know that we are *all* important- and we are all important to God.
-It is important for us to live for others (our children, our family, our fellow man), and God- as well as for ourselves.
-It is important for us all to forgive everyone for everything. Not that we should forget wrongs done, but at any given time, we should forgive everyone- and cleanse our conscience.
-And we should forgive ourselves for everything- everything. And we should cleanse ourselves in that fashion.
-And we should work for what is right. But we have to know right from wrong to do that.
-We must fight, struggle, die- but most important, we must live for what is right. And so, we must know what is justice, or injustice; good, or evil. And you must overthrow what is evil - like this current economic and social system. And you must remove the lies, stupidity, and pseudoscience from psychology. You put pressure on the lies and the weak points. And you see how much stress the materialists psychologists can stand before they crack. And you remind them that they lie about God's creation - and that we live in a causation world. And you see if they understand "if they sow the wind, they might reap the whirl-wind - and it's just about harvest time."
- And you can have an outrageous amount of courage - when you know you are right. So comparatively, fear is defeated. And when you know that the soul is immortal - and it is. Who can harm you, but the Creator?

Let them do whatever God allows them to do with the body. There is even a limit to what can be done against the mind. But you must have faith and trust in our Creator. And you must try to love him back- the way he loves you. And you say, "God's will be done on earth- and in every aspect of my life." And this will help protect you from unwanted effects. But you must remember, many, many circumstances you encounter may not be ones you would consciously select. God will help select conditions for your growth and development. Many of these conditions may seem unpleasant to the ignorant. But they are good for you, if you are into growing.

And then, you can sit back, relax, and watch some fireworks. And enjoy your good health. And Susan, and people really should know this, and they should try this - so we can all be healthy.

# 6 OBSERVATIONS OF THE AUTHOR (VARIOUS)

Content- consists of various personality inventories- or self-analysis

Subject- is the father of Noah.

As mentioned in the observations of Noah, (concerning his parentage), his father was recognized as being "gifted" in his formative years. And he was also an Honors Student in High School. He has been called very talented because of his writings.

A. The MMPI (Minnesota Multiphasic Personality Inventory) and Other Indices

This data speaks for itself, and the language, terms, and descriptions are taken wholly from the MMPI two volume set. The comment on the "L" validity scale is instructive. It is a T score of 56. It says these "values are likely in test subjects who are ministers, reformers, social activists, or evangelical missionaries." I was "called" to the "ministry" on 9/27/94.

The F scale is a 50, and the description "indicates conformity and would indicate few deviant beliefs, attitudes, or unusual experiences, and show a tendency to avoid endorsement of socially unacceptable, threatening, or disturbing content among the test items." My comment would be that is essentially true.

But here are some possible important differences with the materialist psychologists, and their fellow travelers. We believe that dreams and/or visions can be "normal" and useful. We believe in, and know something about "God," as should be the case with all normal human beings. *We believe in the dreams of Jacob, in the dreams of Joseph. We believe in the visions of Daniel, for instance; and we believe in the visions of John, the - Beloved.* From experience, I have a certain sense of the reliability of my own dreams, or visions. And I also know that my own dreams and visions are in conformity with those of our ancestors - that I have just mentioned. And we know that our whole Judeo-Christian-Islamic Tradition, and its real adherents believe essentially I as do. I also say that if the materialists were normal, they also would have dreams or visions, and they would better understand the nature of man.

And if they are not normal, they must be dysfunctional, and abnormal. And if they don't know anything about God, and he's everywhere; again, the materialists must be abnormal. But I will tell you (if we can try to use an analogy), God is more like the weather. And you cannot stop summer, and you cannot stop winter- when it wants to come. You can only adjust to it, and you can study it. And even if you want to study the weather, you better have some respect. And you should realize that God is very much higher than the weather. Again, God is like the Quarterback and the *front four* of the 1985, Chicago

Bears. He will give you the ball. And He will block for you. And you should stay right there "in His back pocket." And you shouldn't try to get ahead of God. For, He will surely block for you. And, when He gives you that ball, you hold it in tight against you to protect it. And you stay in that back pocket until you see some daylight. And then you run, like Walter Payton! And you run over, around, or through anyone (or anything) that gets in your way! And you don't stop until the arms go up, and the cheers go deafening!

And everybody breaks all out in smiles: "Touch down!"

Or, God is like the jab of Muhammad Ali. And he goes rat-a-tat-tat against the nose of devils! And God has even been known to do an "Ali Shuffle" at times. And when the devils get distracted with the jab, or the Ali Shuffle, good people must knock the hell out of them!

Or, on the other hand, good people should keep a stiff left jab in the devils' face, so that when the devils get distracted, God hits them with a Mike Tyson like uppercut, and an overhand right, and knocks the hell out of them! So, you really shouldn't mess around with God! And when people choose God, and choose to do his work, (and to do the right things), and they become God's Chosen, you really should be careful about messing around with them!

And, yes, God is love, and grace, and all of those qualities too. But there comes a time to cut bait. And it is now time to cut bait, to create a world where those qualities will abound in those that are left around. The others will be cut off! And "We" will give them what they have earned!

One of the other problems we have with those materialists is that they lack moral content, or direction. And they do not immediately notice (and state) that an individual opposed to Nazi Germany because of its racism, and inhumanity is not necessarily disordered. The direction of the ruling classes is psychotic!

And if someone in the former Soviet Union is opposed to its materialism, then, he may be healthy, because that society was disordered. And if good people do not, now, stand up, in the USA, and overthrow this materialistic, irrational, destructive, and evil economic, and social order; then they are not healthy.

And if they are intelligent enough to be aware of the disorder here, and have a conscience (and do not stand up for this positive change) - they will probably acquire symptoms of disorder. And the first thing that we must do in that process of affecting change is to rely on, and call upon our God to make the right changes. Then, we will legislate JUBILEE, and other rational, moral precepts listed in "Jubilee Worldwide!" which, see. And the USA will become a place that God (Himself), will be proud of!

On another matter, there is going to be some controversy. But again our guide is our own experience, and our religious documentation: Matthew 11:14 says, "And this I will tell you, if you will make room in your minds, that he is that Elias whose coming was prophesied," in speaking about John, the Baptist. Matthew 17:10 repeats this perspective. So does the Qur'an, but it is done in a different manner. Anyway, I believe in "resurrection," or reincarnation. And this only means that the soul is immortal, minds semi-permanent, and bodies perishable. See the "Resurrection of Noah" for a fuller explanation.

In conclusion, this still makes the validity scales valid. All the remaining material is some true, some partly true, and some not true, in the descriptions.

B. Myers-Briggs Type Indicator

This description is essentially true. I would only add that I am significantly introverted, and strongly intuitive. I am also very much the thinking type. But because of my also outgoing nature, it may not be immediately apparent that I am strongly introverted.

C. Whole Brain Dominance

The individual here possesses Whole Brain Dominance. This means he uses a lot of creativity and imagination. Then, he is very, very thinking, (rational, logical), so he can organize these concepts, or ideas.

It has been observed that the subject here is very fixed, and this is partly true. In some ways, he is very adaptable, very flexible. Much of that is innate. It is like part of the DNA. And much of this has been studied and analyzed in a process where we look at energies. We look at where the power centers are. We look at predispositions. And we correlate this with traditional psychology and other disciplines. We look at how this is used in every day experience. But again, we see things in an affirmative, positive way. "Fixed" may be seen by us also as relentless, solid, stable, consistent, persevering, constant, indomitable, determined, convinced, unwavering, immovable, eternal, etc.

In fact, we see the so-called psychologists' excessive use of negatives, like overcompensate, overachieve, underachieve, etc. as evidence of the fact that the formulators of such terms are, themselves, morbid, negative, and unhealthy. Furthermore, we see this ignorant and faulty attempt to "judge" God's creation as morally wrong and evil. And this may be further evidence that they have been studying rats and other animals too much, and trying to remake man in that image.

The better perspective to use regarding human beings is that they will often "do whatever is necessary to affect a certain outcome." This is because they are made in the image of God, and (should) have creativity, imagination, and reasoning.

One of the things that psychology will learn: people can and do attain balance, harmony, and even maturity within a certain personality type. This would be like a rose maturing and blooming as it has been predisposed, and a lily doing likewise in its domain. And so it is ignorant, even evil to speak of deficits in speaking of either when they don't become each other. Don't try to make a rose a lily, or vice versa. A rose is very content to be a rose.

In other words, a writer may have traits that incline him to develop certain skills that would be different from those of a, say, Michael Jordan. And then, the basketball player, Michael, may not quite have the traits to be a star baseball player.

Also, bigger is not necessarily better. Psychologists speak in terms of "gifted" people being larger than others as if it were a positive (in itself). If bigger were better, then the Tutsi of Burundi should be the masters, or superiors of us all. And where would it leave the Asians, who are generally smaller in stature than Westerners? Consider a Black Hole. It is one of the most powerful forces in the universe. Even light cannot escape its gravitational strength. So, it is concentrated energy. Likewise, human beings (or other objects) may have beauty, intelligence, charisma, logic, grace, poise, strength, speed, argument, a sense of justice, etc. that just holds us spellbound.

So, there are many qualities that are attractive, and powerful. And these don't necessarily depend on size - unless you are a Neanderthal Materialist.

We will bet on King David, over Goliath, any day! And in the Mississippi Delta (where I come from), we were taught, "The bigger they are, the harder they fall!" So, look at the force and power of the individual.

What we find is that people choose a body that will be most effective in doing whatever is sought in a particular lifetime. Even if you are "too" beautiful, it may be a hindrance in a particular environment. And it may distract energies, or efforts from what may be more desirable. And a Mahatma Gandhi (e.g.), will not come into manifestation in the USA, in 1965, (looking like he did in India), and hope to lead the USA very far. Big, (LBJ – Lyndon Johnson ) was the choice.

And a person who dislikes Americans, for instance, might come here (into manifestation) looking like the all-American hero! And you will not suspect the traitor, until he does his evil deed! So, he was just hiding out in the most un-suspecting body available- and waiting for his opportunity. And you will find many Americans like that. For, that is why America is now in such a sad condition.

So, again, this "bigger is better" is one of the ignorant, materialist, pseudoscientific notions that will fall by the wayside. Also with respect to those supposed "gifted" or genius types (and somebody has tested, or ascertained this status) -Why aren't they aware and doing something about changing this society into a just, equitable, and rational society? Could there be something wrong with the tests?

When psychology becomes a real science, it will know:

-Free will is a birthright (right) given to souls throughout the universe. So, they have the right of choosing.
-The purpose of (human) life is for growth, maintenance, and development.
-Souls choose (decide) when, where, and in what human form they will resurrect in. I.e., they decide what ethnic group, nation, community, family, etc., they are to resurrect in.
-Souls choose an environment to resurrect in which is compatible with their level of development, goals, aspirations, needs, wants, and purposes for a particular lifetime. It is more true that souls choose parents, than the other way around. Parents can only invite. Souls choose.

Part of the lesson here is that even though a soul may have the DNA of the parents, he may choose to be opposed to the values and ideology of those parents- because his purposes in that lifetime are in opposition to the purposes of the parents.

- Souls become what they are. i.e., just like a kernel of corn grows into a healthy or weak stalk of corn (it will not, e.g., turn into a tomato); a "good" soul will usually find a way to grow into a "good" and virtuous person. Of course, the reverse also holds true. A scholar will become scholarly. A scumbag will become what he is, even though he is CEO of a Fortune 500 company - or a priest. The manifestation will reflect the environment. I.E., Robin Hood is still an honorable person, though labeled an "outlaw." Malcolm X, even with a criminal record, is honorable.
-The presence of certain kinds, or levels of "intelligence" may actually interfere with the usage of the God-link (which we call Christ) because *choices* made by that individual are in opposition to the "Christ" principles (of sharing, caring, justice, courage). An example of this may be the sociopath, the psychopathic personality, cowards, the selfish, etc.
-Many events that happen to individuals are really "blessings in disguise."
When I got hay fever, at the age of 22, I turned to Yoga. And this helped create the experiences and state of mind to perform my mission in this life. When FDR

got polio, he learned perseverance, courage, a fighting spirit, and empathy for those with problems and difficulties. Look at King David. Look at JFK (and his back injury). Look at Martin Luther King Jr. *Again, if the psychologists want to learn something about people, the first thing that they must learn is that people are all children of God, and they will often do whatever it takes to affect a certain outcome.*

D. Introduction to Dreams and Visions

-Dreams reflect past or future conditions. Whenever dreams meet the "present," they end. Dreams can be "organized" for greater clarity (or realistic, vivid, reflection) by one being more truthful (especially to oneself), and living a more healthy, productive life. Practicing meditation will also increase the clarity and lucidity of dreams and visions.

- "Visions" in healthy individuals are levels of experience sometime during the sleep state, but may be more possible when the mind and body have attained a certain amount of rest or relaxation. Unlike dreams, where sometimes one knows that he is dreaming, in "visions," one is (then and there) conscious of the experience of the vision.

Depending on the state of the individual, visions may contain high levels of energy. The subject matter of visions here, just like conscious experiences, cover a wide spectrum. They may involve objects, people, events, or places. And they may involve taking part in activities.

When there is greater energy, there is usually greater clarity and/or understanding of what lesson(s) are to be learned. But, many experiences here, just like conscious experiences, have apparent limited usefulness. And like dreams, visions seem to only reflect past, or future "events." Visions seem to be a more direct interaction with what we would call spiritual forces, because, even though in a kind of sleep state, we are "conscious." And there is always the presence of moving energies. The prophets have generally described these as "winds," or seeming moving "flames," etc.

-Dreams and visions are a reminder that we are all like our Father, God. For, we were made in His image. He is Omniscient, Omnipotent, and Omnipresent. He is time. He is timeless. We live and have our "being" in Him. We are part of Him.

If we are righteous, in dreams or visions, we experience wondrous things. We can learn things that have escaped our conscious notice. We can have confirmation of beliefs. We can see the possibility of "future" events.

E. Time, Space, and God

These aspects are more fully dealt with in the section, "What's On Your Mind?" which, see.

In closing, the evolutionary level of individuals will be reflected by heredity, and their environment. But souls have chosen environments and DNA options (bodies) that correspond to what they are, and what they want, or need to accomplish in a particular lifetime.

There is much that is useful in psychology and psychiatry. But much of the theories and ideas are like those of someone partially color blind, and just entering puberty, but deciding what imagery, love and life are all about. Freud, Jung, and Adler are examples. Freud contributed much, but even Jung and Adler were more advanced in many ways. Jung may have been the more advanced. But Jung, himself, was not whole (or integrated within himself). And that is why he did so poorly in finding real solutions, or getting a full understanding. So, the "mind sciences" need to become focused- and grow up.

We should recognize that while left, or right brain dominance may be useful for concentration, or rigorous specialization- they probably don't (can't see the big picture).

And we must start with the basics. I have discussed these in "What's On Your Mind?" And we must approach the study of God's creations with proper respect- which is not the case, now. The motivations must be correct!

Then, I believe that "good," healthy, normal people, with normal, or above intelligence, with "whole brain dominance" ( possibly, the "Mother of All Brains"), and "O Positive blood (possibly, the Mother of All Blood), and Unity within themselves can find better solutions to whatever problems we have- because the DNA might be "better."

I believe people with Unity can often use skill beyond the intellect, or what we call insight, or intuition (in a conscious, or dream state). It seems to be a more direct interaction with what we call the Christ-link. And, when it is the higher mind, it is the truth-or God. It will make perfect sense. It will be rational, logical, just, beautiful, obvious. So, we should locate, and make maximum use of people who have these qualities.

Finally, it should be noted that the author has practiced a variation of yoga, since 1971, and this has affected the quality (clarity) of his dreams, and/or visions.

Prospects? We shall see.

# 7 HEALTHY PSYCHOLOGICAL INVENTORIES

(An Example, Using Test Results From The MMPI)

Indices of Psychology

1. Number of scales with T score over 70 —none

2. Number of scales between T score of 40 and 60—8 of 13

3. Disturbance Index (DsI)—461.78, where 550 and above is used to determine significant degrees of disturbance are present. 549 and below are called normal adjustment.

| | |
|---|---|
| a. L – 0 | j. Pt - 2.7 |
| b. F – (-25.2) | k. Sc - 3.6 |
| c. K – 178 | l. Ma - 49.8 |
| d. Hs - 0 | m. Si - 4.7 |
| e. D – 43 | n. A - 2.38 |
| f. Hy - 17.8 | o. R - 0 |
| g. Pd - 69.6 | p. Es - 37.4 |
| h. Mf - 42.4 | _____ |
| i. Pa - 35.6 | DsI - 461.78 |

4. Mt (maladjustment) Raw score is 2, T score is 34.12

5. SOC (social adjustment) Raw score is 2, T score is 36.

6. Index of psychopathology ((Ip) on a scale of 1 to 10, it is 3.5 )
   Ip =.1Pa+ .06Sc- 6.26=3.5).

7. Indices in Leary's interpersonal diagnostic system.

   a. DOM (dominance) is 2 (i.e., DOM vs. submissiveness)

   b. LOV (love) is 39 (i.e. love vs. hate).

8. Other Indices

   a. AI (anxiety index) is 42.66

   b. A (anxiety, first factor) is 35

   c. At (Iowa manifest anxiety) is 34.72

   d. R (repression (repression, second factor) is 53

   e. Repression, factor scale II is 43

   f. IR (internalization ratio) is .863

   g. HOS ( manifest hostility) is 37

   h. Hostility, Finney, is 35.43

   i. Hostility, McDougall, is 33.81.

   j. REL (religious fundamentalism) is 49.

   k. PSY (psychoticism) is 45.

   l. PHO (phobias) is 35.

   m. Autocratic (power) is 21 (i.e., leader vs. follower).

   n. DEP (depression) is 38.

   o. K is 68

   p. ES (ego strength) is 67.

9. Validity Scales

a. L - 56 (moderate elevation). Elevated scale values are likely in test subjects who are ministers, reformers, social activists, or evangelical missionaries.

b. F - 50 (middle range). This indicates conformity and would indicate few deviant beliefs, attitudes, or unusual experiences and shows a tendency to avoid endorsement of socially unacceptable, threatening or disturbing test items.

c. K - 68 (moderately elevated). A low K is associated with the psychotic tetrad (scales 2, 4, 6, 8). A high K is associated with the neurotic triad (scales 2, 3, 4). Scorer in high average (57-64) is well adjusted, self-reliant, and easily capable of dealing with everyday problems.

There seems to be few emotional disturbances or threats to self-esteem or self-control and little interpersonal wrangling. These persons show restraint, prudence, and circumspection in their everyday conduct and behavior. Also:

| | |
|---|---|
| reasonable | ingenious |
| clear thinking | enthusiastic |
| showing initiative | verbal |
| readily ego-involved | sociable |
| enterprising | being a good mixer |
| resourceful | taking an ascendant role |
| versatile | having wide interests and fluent |

having high intellectual ability

These men were competent, effective, and well balanced. There is no implication that they were not concerned about their own personal or social status, rather they are quite content with the way they find themselves.

Moderately elevated scores (65-74) indicated efforts to maintain an appearance of adequacy, control, and effectiveness.

10. Basic Scales

a. Scale #1 is 49, low (Hs) Hypochondrias

Friends described men as having narrow interests and the women as being well balanced and conventional. Adjectives typifying were:

| | |
|---|---|
| alert | argumentative |
| quick to adjust | intelligent |
| at ease in oral expression | outgoing |
| cheerful | having initiative |
| capable | persuasive |
| good-looking | competitive |
| responsible | warm |

The general picture seems to be one of freedom from hampering, neurotic inhibitions, from over evaluation of oneself and one's own problems, and from undue concern about adverse reactions of others. These persons are also characterized by an energetic and spontaneous pursuit of the goals and aims in which they have a sincere interest and investment. In the self-reports of the men, only the descriptions sensitive, emotional, and soft hearted appeared in the analysis.

b. Scale #2 is 44, low (D) Depression

Lower scores reflect a naturalness, buoyancy, and freedom of thought and action that lead to easy social relations, confidence in taking on tasks and effectiveness in a variety of activities. The lack of inhibition in low 2's may, in certain contexts lead to negative reactions from others, however, as a result of hurt feelings, slighted friendships, and threatened confidences. Men are seen by their peers as balanced, self-controlled, self-confident. Also:

| active | good natured | adventurous |
| hardheaded | affected | humorous |
| aggressive | impulsive | alert |
| informal | autocratic | intelligent |
| cheerful | outgoing | egotistical |
| outspoken | emotional | quick |
| energetic | responsible | enthusiastic |
| restless | excitable | self-seeking |
| generous | prone to show off | spontaneous |
| witty | talkative | having initiative |

c. Scale #3 is 62, high (Hy) Hysteria

The adjectives describing the males were:

| | | |
|---|---|---|
| fair minded | energetic | persevering |
| enthusiastic | prone to worry | assertive |
| enterprising | socially forward | alert |
| adventurous | generous | affectionate |
| mature | sentimental | clear thinking |
| cooperative | talkative | good tempered |
| kind | grateful | individualistic |
| verbal | mix well socially | courageous |
| have wide interests | | |

Judges rated high males:

| | | |
|---|---|---|
| clever | inhibited | enterprising |
| enthusiastic | spunky | imaginative |
| infantile | impatient | thankless |
| both responsible and irresponsible | | independent in judgment |
| high degree intellective ability | | ability to think for themselves |

The psychological picture is one of social participation and easy accessibility, ready involvement in activities, and participation in social activities.

d. Scale #4 is 58, high (Pd) Psychopathic Deviate

These persons are adventurous and courageous, sociable in both senses of the word (socially forward and mixing well), talkative and verbal, enthusiastic, good tempered. frank, generous, fair minded, and individualistic. Also, said to have wide interests and like drinking. They are characterized as sensitive and prone to worry. They are described by their peers as hostile and aggressive in their interpersonal relationships, sarcastic and cynical, as well as ostentatious and exhibitionistic. IPAR assessed this type as tense, moody, nervous, and resentful, aggressive, immature, irritable, leisurely, and unemotional.

e. Scale #5 is 61, high (Mf) Masculinity-femininity

These persons were characterized by their peers as sensitive and prone to worry, idealistic and peaceable, sociable and curious, and having general aesthetic interests. IPAR described these as psychologically complex and inner directed, intellectually able and interested. They were seen to value cognitive pursuits and to derive important satisfactions from such work and achievements. They showed concern with philosophical problems, but not necessarily in only an abstract, disinterested way. They frequently took stands on moral issues and at times showed a great deal of self-awareness and self-concern that was neither neurotic, nor immature. They were seen as socially perceptive and responsive to interpersonal nuances; these attributes showed up as good judgment and common sense.

f. Scale #6 is 67, high (Pa) Paranoia

Males with high scores were rated as sensitive, emotional, and prone to worry. They were seen as kind, affectionate, generous, and grateful. Also, sentimental, and softhearted, peaceable, cooperative, and courageous and as having wide interests. IPAR raters saw them as readily becoming ego-involved, and tending to make these pursuits personally relevant and important. Also, energetic and industrious, and as showing high initiative, poised, rational, and clear thinking, intelligent, and insightful, with wide interests and progressive approaches. Self-descriptions were trustful, amorous, and worldly.

g. Scale #7 is 58, high (Pt) Psychasthenia

Peer raters found these sentimental, peaceable, and good tempered. Also verbal, individualistic, and dissatisfied. IPAR found these to be dull, formal, and unemotional. Also, idealistic, and insightful; appeared immature and quarrelsome. Self-descriptions were sentimental and high strung with general aesthetic interests and national, political interests.

h. Scale #8 is 51, high (Sc) Schizophrenia

These were rated as prone to worry, self-dissatisfied and conscientious, good tempered, versatile, and enthusiastic with wide interests and general aesthetic interests. Also, frank, fair-minded, and courageous. Appeared kind and sentimental, as well as peaceable. IPAR found them effective in communicating their ideas clearly, but showing evidence of being at odds with themselves and of having major internal conflicts. Also, hostile, blustery, irritable, resentful, touchy, moody, stubborn, opinionated, autocratic, deceitful, disorderly, and impulsive. They displayed imaginative, mischievous, and sharp-witted behavior. Self-descriptions include high strung, conscientious, worrying, individualistic, enterprising, adventurous, curious, and amorous; also, frank, talkative, kind, sentimental and grateful.

i. Scale #9 is 55, high (Ma) Hypomania

Peer ratings include adjectives sociability, energy, openness, forward, talkative, and verbal, individualistic, impulsive, enthusiastic, adventurous, and curious, with interest in national, political matters. Also, liking drinking, generous, softhearted, affectionate and sentimental. Acquaintances described as prone to worry, self-dissatisfied, and conventional. IPAR found these sensitive, thoughtful, and imaginative, as anxious and nervous, and as deceitful and unfriendly. Self-descriptions include impulsive, talkative, adventurous, liking to drink, frank, and reclusive.

j. Scale #10 is 37, low (Si) Social Introversion

These were seen as social and versatile in the sense of mixing well. Also, expressive, ebullient, colorful persons. They tended to be ostentatious and exhibitionistic, active, vigorous and competitive with their peers. They showed strong initiative and took the ascendant role in relations with others. They appeared to possess high intellectual ability and were verbally fluent and facile. They were persuasive and often won others over to their viewpoint. They also manipulated others in attempting to gain their own ends, seeing things rather opportunistically rather than sensitive to the meaning and value of these persons as individuals.

These men were seen as potentially guileful and deceitful. They emphasized oral pleasure in a self-indulgent way, seeking aesthetic and sensuous impressions. They appeared unable to delay gratification and often acted with insufficient thought and deliberation. This under control of their impulses, combined with their tendency to get ego involved in many different things, led to a characteristic aggressiveness or hostility in their personal relations.

These men emphasized success and productive achievement as a means for achieving status, recognition, and power. They readily become counterproductive in the face of frustration and easily aroused hostility and resentment in those with whom they dealt. IPAR found them active, ambitious, and blustery. Also, immature, hasty, quick, ingenious, witty, and having initiative. Self-descriptions include sociable, enterprising, enthusiastic, affectionate and responsive, courageous and cheerful, hardheaded, facing life, temperate, and adaptable.

# 8 MYERS – BRIGGS TYPE INDICATOR – THE INTJ TYPE

(Notice how the different test descriptions of personality reinforce each other).

The introverted intuitive is the outstanding innovator in the field of ideas, principles, and systems of thought. He trusts his own intuitive insight as to the true relationships and meanings of things, regardless of established authority or popularly accepted beliefs. His faith in his inner vision of the possibilities is such that he can remove mountains - and often does. In the process, he may drive others, or oppose them, as hard as his own inspirations drive him. Problems only stimulate him; the impossible takes a little longer, but not much.

His outer personality is judging, being mainly due to his auxiliary, which is T. Thus, he backs up his original insight with the determination, perseverance and enduring purpose of a judging type. He wants his ideas worked out in practice, applied and accepted, and spends any time and effort necessary to that end.

The danger for the type arises from his single-minded concentration. He sees his goal so clearly that he may miss other things that he ought to see, even though they conflict with that goal: the rights, interest, feelings and points of view of other people; facts, conditions and counter forces that do exist and must be reckoned with. He should talk over his plans with an extroverted sensing type and really listen to him.

He is outstandingly effective in scientific research and engineering design where his boldly ingenious ideas have to meet and fit reality. He always needs some such reality-check, but the very boldness of his ideas may be of immense value in any field and should not be smothered in a routine job full of details.

If his judgment is undeveloped, he cannot criticize his own inner vision, and he tends to reject judgments from outside without really hearing them. As a result, he cannot shape his inspirations into effective action, and may appear only as a visionary, or crank.

He is the "most individualistic and most independent of all the types."

Resembles extroverted thinker, both in his organizing ability and in the danger of ignoring other peoples' feelings and views.

Needs to make a real effort to understand and appreciate.

Likely to be an effective, relentless organizer. Can be an efficient executive, rich in ideas. The INTJ's usually have original minds and great drive for their own ideas and purposes.
In the fields that appeal to them, they have a fine power to organize a

job and carry it through with, or without help. Skeptical, critical, independent, determined, sometimes stubborn. They must learn to yield less important points in order to win the most important.

# 9 DO DREAMS REFLECT ANY REALITY?
### (Some Examples)

The following are some dreams that the author had about his son:

1). Had dream about Noah on morning of 9/21/94. He said, "They're trying to drown me, Jimmy Lee." This has something to do with a real or potential (past, current, or future) threat to his safety or well-being. Also, he was a baby (about 3-6 months old) in the dream. I was with Tonya. And to me, (in the dream) I was simply impressed by the fact that he could speak.

2). On 6/25/93, dream that indicated that his name, or role was that of "Valencia," or "Valence," which means a "bond."

3). On 1/31/93, I had a vision about "Joseph Jr., Negro." That name was in a "book" structure. While I was trying to read what was said about "JJR," there was something like the sound of thunder, a bell, explosion (all at once), etc., and I awoke.

4). In about February, I had a dream where he was unclad from the waist down, and he was crying (loudly). I had (have) never had another dream about a child of mine crying before.

5). In about April, I had a dream where it was stated that his *IQ was 200*, on about Wednesday, or Thursday. On the next Sunday, I saw a program on CBS's Sunday Morning about a 12.5 year old named Masoud, who had an *IQ of 200!* Masoud had finished college and had planned to enter Medical School. (His parents were, respectively, of Iranian, and Mexican backgrounds).

In the dream, Noah was about 3-4 years old. He had numerous freckles. His navel was a little big. He had big (beautiful) eyes. Earlier, in the dream, Tonya was about 7-9 years old, and said, "I want my mommy, I want my mommy." Then, Noah had appeared. There was also a reference to Jimmy Jr. in the first part of the dream.

6). In the next dream, Noah was with Runako and I as we washed a van. He wanted, he insisted that Runako kiss him, now, immediately. He started crying, in his impatience.

7). The next dream indicated that Tonya's current role in his life ended, and was replaced by input from me.

8). The next dream was about Noah when he was about 6-7 months old. He had on two-toned (of two colors) shoes. Robert (his cousin), was in the background. He was "walking rings around" Robert. Robert was not walking.

9). Had dream about Noah on the morning of 10/9/94. He was really sick with a cold. Nose was visibly stopped-up, severely. Maybe, eyes seemed affected. I held him and got down on my knees and prayed for God to help him. Note: In real life, Noah did get sick with a cold on Sunday night, Monday morning, about 2:30 A.M., according to Judy. He has had a problem with a cold since then, though not so severe, sometimes.

10). On 10/24/94, I had a dream in the morning about Noah. He seemed OK. No complaints. Seemed healthy, satisfied. Seems that I kissed him on the cheek, hugged his face.

11). There was a previous dream that involved Noah (maybe). Saw a youngster using crayons on the wall. It was, is not clear that that was Noah.

12). 11/1/94. Had dream about Noah today. We were playing. Seems that he had something on his head; maybe a headband, or some kind of hat, or cap. I was later, playfully trying to get his attention, or get him to do something. He kind of ignored me, like he won't look at you sometimes. Noah did seem happy in this latest dream.

13). 12/10/94. Dream about Noah wanting, or asking for baby oil on his face(?)

14). 1/10/95. Dream about Noah being with Gloria and I. We were in bed together. I believe Noah was singing.

15). 1/11/95. Had dream of Noah. He was walking.

16). 6/7/95. Dreamed of Noah and his cold(s). I was telling someone that he never had these before about 9/21/94. Noah came over and kissed me. I hugged and picked him up. There is something about a door being open, where a draft was possibly a source of, or creating the cold(s).

17). 6/25/95. Had dream about Noah where he was very dark complexioned. He was smiling.

# 10 INTRODUCTION TO DREAMS AND VISIONS

The following are visions and dreams of the author. But before we get into that, here are three important concepts:

1). *The Second Coming of Christ* has already been described (set forth) by the prophets. And it is a great, massive learning that will take place, as the old systems fall, and new ones need to be ushered in for humanity to even survive on the earth plane.

At such time, those who have prepared themselves for the leadership of the new age will receive visions, visitations, and channelings from that God-link who has become known as the Christ. And, as these simultaneously occur throughout the network of those who have taken upon themselves this leadership of the new age, there will be this Christ Consciousness of such a vibrational level that it may be deemed The Second Coming, or the Unity. And we expect to see very interesting events over the next 3.5 years

2). The definition of Satan, or the devil is the quality, misuse, or wrongful use of energies. It is selfishness, greed, envy, jealousy, hatred, lying, oppression, etc. And we have defined it many times. (See *This World Is Mine* and *The Resurrection of Noah* for a fuller definition). And those who have those attributes, we call devils.

3). "Hooking Up" with God means using the Christ-Link. The best way to use it is for "spiritual goals." An environment that is too structured may inhibit its effectiveness. There should be an intellectual and experiential effort to relinquish control to God. Say, "God's will be done in all aspects of my life." Then, you must apply those principles.

If you don't apply lessons learned, their value is diminished. The urgings, creativity, imagination, and reasoning will flow in a process of *naturalness*. Watch superior, instinctive, athletes (or musicians). Consider the martial arts. The effect is almost like driving with cruise control. You basically just steer a little, and go along for the ride.

Again, consider how the multitudes were fed with just a few fishes. You must have love, faith, and trust in Our Father. And you must have courage.

Beware pseudo Christians and Muslims. Many are ignorant, hypocrites, phonies, and devils. They say one thing, but do another. Beware the Sadducees (materialists). Know that the body can be good and divine, when in unity with God. Sex, when in love, is divine. And moderation is usually best for you.

Do not go on a guilt trip like the silly pseudo-Christians, and call God's creation negative things. And know that Islam can be used with Christianity to give a balanced presentation on many matters.

We are indeed back, because God is today reclaiming the earth from the devils. They were allowed a certain period of rule. *Their system has been weighed in the balance and found wanting. Their time is up!*

# 11 THE DREAMS AND VISIONS

1). 7/31/1971. I saw Aunt Hattie, Aunt Bessie, Uncle Son, and another man accompanying, it seems, Aunt Hattie in a boat (at a dock). In retrospect, perhaps they were posing for a picture. The men had gray hair. The picture was later put on the front page of "The Defender" Newspaper.

Aunt Hattie had come into some monetary resources which resulted in many people (Caucasians, African Americans, and others), coming to her and forming an (apparently) protest, or demonstration, type group. And I was thinking that this group was a more or less ideal, ready-made group, that as a start, would launch what actions I was to pursue in the way of activist type programs.

These people, it seemed, had found their way to her door and were gathered outside (partly) as a result, or consequence, of Aunt Hattie's popularity, or resources. The boat, to back track, was, of course, sitting in water, but there was nothing extraordinary about the water. The gray hair made a deep imprint.

Vision

2). Sometime near, but prior to 5/11/81, "I saw myself having a good flow of green' healing power coming from my fingers."

Dream

3). 2/12/1985. "I was with Gloria. I had an approximately 5-month-old son. He was very handsome."

Visions

4). "On about 4/5/72, I had a vision where I was deflecting two rays of current deployed by a bearded, groveling, Caucasian antagonist. Then there was the presentation of a triangle. Then, there was the presentation of two additional triangles."

5). "4/13/72. I saw several images, after an experience that began with a swishing, bulk of whitish energy. The most outstanding of which was an upside down skull, displayed a long while, and most vividly."

6). "4/16/72. I saw 3 or 4 presentations of a skull (right side up) first, two together. Then, one with flesh on it, which then disintegrated down to a skull...."

7). 10/2/73. I saw a figure's head, which seemed to have a wreath, with a flower, displayed prominently. The presentation was like a drawing. It seemed like a man's head.

Dreams

8). 10/27/72. The only remembrance is of water, in a great quantity. I was concerned lest the water, which came in the form of rain, would flood my basement. (To me, water denotes spirituality). I suspect that I have a fear that the spirituality that I am 'showered' with will cause me some disadvantage. I must erase that fear, if it exists. And, I will have to summon perpetual courage to dig deep into the psyche, into the subconscious, so that it may be reconstructed.

9). 11/8/72. I traveled this railroad train (a dream I've had a number of times before). The tracks run from what (from a Chicago viewpoint) would be southeast to northwest. I have caught the train many times underground at the loop, going in the northwest(?) direction.

One has to go under, over, and along the tracks, to board the train. I also traveled several underground, or ground level roads to get to the boarding place.

At one point I came to the entrance of one which said "downtown." I realized I was going in the wrong direction when I saw this. Most of the time, the route to the boarding area was only peopled by me, or sparsely peopled.

10). 11/10/72. Had dream over at Washington's store, or another building at that approximate location. Dream was about Gloria's brother (who lived on Christiana). He had gone to Spain to escape being jailed. And in the dream, he came to the door of the building across the street. He seemed to have had his hair "blown" (i.e. made to seem more like the Spanish). His complexion was light brown, and I thought that this would enable him to blend well with the 'dark' complexioned Spanish people.

Visions

11). August, 1972. Just before the customary season that I get hay fever, I had the following vision: Out back of the house that Aunt Bessie lived in in Drew, Mississippi was a raised wooden platform. I sat on it and was astonished to be able to see the inner portion of my body- basically, the upper chest area, (perhaps), lungs, spinal area, liver, pancreas, stomach, and heart. The organs were pulsating (active). In the vision, I was happy to discover that I was able to see the inner, working- the metabolic processes of myself. I (in the vision-dream) then headed back toward the house where there was a large 4 ft. diameter pot in the front yard. I think it had water in it.

12). 11/13/72. I had the first experience with a great amount of energy involved since before the hay fever season. There was a stream of energy which lasted for, it seemed, three minutes. Then, at or near the end, I saw a partial, or full figure of a man with a mustache. His skin was colorless, or white, almost like a drawing. Then, at the end of the energy, there was a large figure of a man, head only, to the left-peripheral. His hair was black, or brown, and his skin was Caucasian. He was alive-like, but I recall no particular expression (that he bore).

The first man seemed alive, too. The beam of energy was very pleasant, and I was still, hopefully, waiting for more, when I realized that it had expended all the force that I was to receive at that intensity level. The beam of energy is still directed to the head area. It still seems to come from without. At the end of the force, there is usually a presentation of an object, seen as one would watch an object on the TV screen.

There was an area (1 X 1.5 inches) on the last figure's face above the right side that became exposed to what is under the skin- like the encyclopedic method of 'see-through' exposures of the human body (after the initial few seconds of presentation).

13). 6/14/82. Vision where I saw portions of central, southern, west-central Africa, and also the West/North central USA. Names/words were not very intelligible, discernible.

14). 1/13/1981. I had a vision-dream about being Japanese during the time when there was a war against the Catholics , or about 1637. I was a soldier, had (acne). I was about 25 years of age, had on a soldier's uniform.

15). About 9/6/93. I was traveling over an area similar to the "Grand Canyon." I felt the kind of love that emanates from God during the experience. It is superior to anything or anyone that we know of. It makes everything, and everyone else seem subordinate to that power/feeling, purity, divinity, righteousness.

16). 4/27/79. I went deep, deep into the subconscious, enroute, seeing one or two lighted objects (experience similar to looking into the heavens on a dark night). The objects seemed not so distant as planets, or stars. Then, I decided that I would find out what (a certain person was doing). So, I spun around (the effect appeared so) COUNTERCLOCKWISE, ended up in a place with mostly women. I didn't find the person I was looking for. My energy level decreased and the vision wound down.

17). About February, 1993. I had two recent visions about the "Eye of Providence." First, it was there, and observed by me. Second, I seemed to have it merge into me.

18). On morning of 5/4/93, at about 4:50 A.M. It seemed that there were two beings (men). They were somewhat disguised as ordinary, interacting with individuals or groups (like in a school room setting). One, then became a preacher, a minister. He was at the rostrum. He was saying that to be a "dreamer" is a noble, worthwhile state, or endeavor. He looked (while giving the lecture- sermon) somewhat like a lion, with long streams of hair (almost white) surrounding his head. To emphasize his point, he then leaned his radiant head forward and levitated about 5-6 feet off the floor. I then awoke.

19). Morning of 10/4/93. Had vision about a 'cube' of white energy that came to our home and intersected, merged into the 'living room' where Tonya and I were. I told her that we were very special people, and in the vision, I was aware of the time that we (she and I) had seen the 'unidentified object' (unusual lights) in the fields southeast of our house on about 4/19/84.

20). On 9/27/94, at about 4:30 P.M., I was called to the ministry in a fashion similar to Samuel's "calling." I was called, by name, 3 times, with a slight variation each time, while in an almost sleep, or restful state. I later videotaped, at our Access TV Station, selections from "Resurrection," and other productions. There was an actual power failure as I was recording, when "Witnesses" tried to connect to Commonwealth Edison (light). I later used my (car) headlights at our Town center to light the way for 'Dawn,' et al., (who provide food and sustenance to people"). Note: Headlights here, are seen as "the light of the head- or the enlightened mind."

Dreams

21). 4/5/1981. Dream involving test which may show a different cell structure (in myself). Perhaps, an alignment, or "conjunction" of the outer electrons.

22). About 7/30/82. "I had an interesting dream about two beautiful women. One had very long hair; both were beautiful, brown, one more smooth. The dream concerned males coming from male sperm, women from hair (rib) protein."

23). About 1/30/93, had dream about Shaheen (a co-worker). She was very beautiful, but did not look as she looks in this lifetime. She was telling another girl (woman) that the thought, or act of kissing or (necking) made her feel kind of queasy, (yucky), embarrassed, ill at ease, maybe because the feeling seemed to control her, or exist independently of her wishes. She was smiling, laughing about it. Shaheen had a very beautiful, but hooked (Indian, Semitic(?)) nose.

24). "2/10/93. Had dream last night about my son. He was a baby, but could hum, or make sounds that created a melody." Note: At this time, I did not have a son, in the flesh.

25). "3/28/93. Another dream about a son. Seems that Gloria was the mother. It was kind of a dream within a dream. In the dream, I knew that I had dreamed about that child, or that incident. She had him first; handed him off to me."

26). "About 4/12/93. I put a gun on an individual; I tried to fire it, but it did not fire. Then, I kicked the individual down stairs, into an object, in a vicious, brutal assault. Note: This is not like me in this life(?). There was another dream showing this kind of relentless attack (which, details I do not recall now). Moral: We all need to ask for forgiveness, and mercy, and also give it."

27). "5/21/93. I dreamed I was in the Air Force, with rank A1C."

28). "On about 9/26/1992. I had a dream where I was playing guitar. Then, I began to play (with instinct, perhaps), and the playing became superior and effortless. Note: I have never played guitar, in this lifetime.

The above are just some of the dreams, or visions of the author. A lot of them that were omitted are about sons, other family members, or relatives. Other omitted ones have romantic, or sexual content. And many just seem of very limited (if of any) value. Some might just be inappropriate, especially, at this time. But, dreams can be useful. And for normal human beings, dreams or visions are normal. And if one does not remember his dreams, we should be asking, "Why?"

# 12 HOW'S YOUR ENERGY LEVEL?

In February of 1994, I noticed some curious instances of what I call energy functionality - or the interaction of energy forces based on the electromagnetic, gravitational, and nuclear forces inherent in individuals, or other bodies with mass. I noticed that I was surrounded at work by many instances of what I view as reflections (or similarities), or opposites, as follows:

A. Seeing Double: Jimmie Lee Meets Jimmie Lee

1. There was a fellow worker named Jimmie Lee Robinson, who, I believe, was born in Arkansas. That is exactly *the* name I was born with, across the Mississippi River, in Mississippi.

2. I was born when the sun traveled through the astronomical sign of Gemini; he, when it traveled through the opposite sign, Sagittarius.

3. "Jimmie Lee" had two sons about the ages of my two daughters. One son worked with him at this company, as has one of my daughters. We drove the same color automobile. And, of course, we did the same kind of work.

B. Am I Reflected Here, Or What?

I encountered numerous instances of functionality that involve a Gemini female, born on the 4th of June, 1971, with the sun being in just about the exact same position as it was when I was born. (I was born 6/3/1944).

2 a. She started work in that location on 1/13/94.

2b. I started work in that location on 1/31/94.

3a. She lived about 4 miles from Forest Park.

3b. I live about 4 miles from Park Forest.

4a. She went to an all girl's high school.

4b. I went to an all boy's high school.

5a. She played flute in High School.

5b. I played clarinet in High School.

6a. She had twin sisters.

6b. I have a "twin brother," i.e., one with the same name as I.

7. The year we were born is the year of a 9 (i.e. 1+9+4+4=18=1+8=**9**; 1971 likewise=9).

8. We regularly listened to the same news radio station, WBBM (News radio, Chicago)

9. Her father was named Joseph, which is one of my names. And we know that a woman's partner is a reflection of her father- just as the opposite is true for a man.

10. She very much identified with her predominate ethnic heritage, as do I.

11. Other symbolic correspondences were as follows:

a. Her sun was in the 10th house; my moon was in the 10th house (The sun and moon are considered complements. And the sun, for a woman is analogous to the moon, for a man).

b. Part of the greatest force of our respective being was in Aquarius and Gemini.

c. Both Ascendants were earthy- hers Virgo, mine Capricorn.

d. The evolutionary time symbol matched (i.e., she was 22 years old, a 4; I, 49 = 4).

C. And Here is a List of Other Symbols:

| **Her** | **My** |
|---|---|
| 1. ☉ △ ♂ | ☉ ✶ ♂ |
| 2. ☉ △ North Node | ☉ ☌ POF |
| 3. ☉ △ ♅ | ☉ ☌ ♅ |
| 4. ☉ 13 deg. ♊; Asc 12 deg. ♍ | ☉ 13 deg. ♊; Asc 15 ♑ |
| 5. ☿ ☌ ♀ ♉ | ☿ ♉, ♊, in mutual dep. |
| 6. ☿ 25 deg. ♉ | ☿ 19 deg. ♉ |
| 7. ☿ ☍ ♃ | ☿ □ ♃ |
| 8. ♀ △ ♇ | ♀ ✶ ♇ |
| 9. ♀ □ ♂ | ♀ ✶ ♂ |
| 10. ♂ △ ♅ | ♂ ✶ ♅ |
| 11. ♇ ✶ ♆ | ♇ ✶ ♆ |
| 12. ♄ ☍ ♆ | ♄ □ ♆ |
| 13. ☉ in 10th | ☽ in 10th |

Also, I was in ROTC, the Air Force, and continue to be much interested in non-fiction related military strategies, tactics and other similar matters. The Gemini's father was a career military person; and he, like I, will still (respect- fully) wear a military shirt.

### D. Other Coworkers Show Reflection Too

There was another co-worker named David Lee, who had come from Korea, possibly 10 years previously. He played guitar (instead of a harp) and he had two or more guitars. He had some association with those in the martial arts (the science of war), of which I am very interested in. And David Lee worked alongside a master in martial arts at this company.

So, following the realization of the above, I looked more closely at my home surroundings.

1. My name is Jacob, Jimmie, James.

2. I live at an numerical address equivalent to that famous *144,000* mentioned in our religious documents. And those numbers = a 9.

3. I was born in 1944-the year of a 9.

4. I was born 6/3/1944, the day of a 9.

5. I live in a town named in part for the university that resides there. To my left is a school. To my right is a library, and a school. And schools, libraries, and universities are places that hold or impart knowledge, or enlightenment (which is "light"). So, symbolically, I am in the mist of light. And since energy will vibrate at, or create vibrations in its environment to match its inherent nature, I RADIATE LIGHT, AND I SOAK UP LIGHT, I impart light, just like the light bearer! And we do this on a grand, expansive scale, because the 9 is also a symbol for Jupiter. And, just like iron filings will align themselves with the flow of radiation, or current, so do we. For again, we are electromagnetic, and when we have real substance, our strength of gravity, and electromagnetism will be relentless; we will align with, or we shall be aligned.

We use other symbols, or configurations to understand where power and energy are stored.

Using my date of birth, we devise the following configuration. It consists of the symbol for Jupiter, at the top, opposite the moon symbol. Symbols for Mercury and mars are present.

-Jupiter represents (Sagittarius) the self, or ego here. And it would be opposite Gemini, as mentioned previously.

6 -3 -1944 = 9

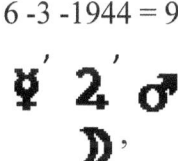

Figure #1

-As mentioned above, my residence is a 9. Across the street is its opposite, an upside down 9, or a 6, because these numbers reflect each other. And recall that we live in a world where if we identify west, we also create an east - opposites.

So, the individual living at the "6" has a name which means "celebrated, poetic prophet" (a reflection of me), because he is not a writer, or poet.

-Sagittarius means he who has "vision." The opposite of vision is "blind." So, my neighbor to my left is actually blind. And he is a minister.

-We also saw (in Figure #1) that Jupiter is opposite the symbol for females-the moon. And my neighbors to my right are actually all females, and reflect other relevant variables.

When I first noticed these correspondences, I thought that they would help prove that God exists because they seem to be an indication that we are usually where we are supposed to be in our evolution- or even our address. And the order seen here indicates that intelligence, structure, reliability, and even balance prevails in God's universe. Wherever, we are, we could possibly belong there.

Another thing to learn about energies can be shown by looking at another configuration, again, based on the date of birth. And the reason that we use the date of birth is that all mass radiates energies. When a human comes into manifestation, he comes at a time and place, when (and where) energy quality and quantity reflect his level of evolutionary development of spirit, body, and mind. So, there will be compatibility between the person being born and the energies then present- on various levels. And we have symbols that help give insight into understanding what those energies are. It is important to remember that symbols are not energies. And the energies themselves may be difficult to measure, except the effect of them.

Note that there is "male" energy in females, and vice versa. And the "energy" may be present, but if there is no way to release it, it is not apparent.

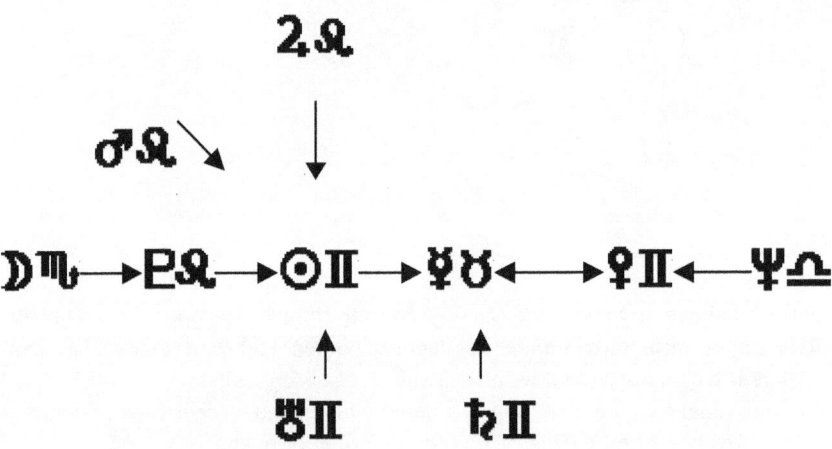

Figure #2

Figure #2 shows how energies give, take, and share resources, space, and time.

|  | Fire | Earth | Air | Water |
|---|---|---|---|---|
| Cardinal-<br>(1 planet) |  |  | ♆ 1.5 |  |
| Fixed- 5 planets | ♂ 7<br>♇ 8<br>♃ 20 | ☿ 20 |  | ☽ 11 |
| Mutable-<br>(4 planets) |  |  | ☉ 13<br>♅ 9<br>♀ 7<br>♄ 28 |  |
|  | 3 | 1 | 5 | 1 |

Figure #3

The configuration above (of the author) shows that individual energies (or humans) seek an environment that complements, or reinforces places of relative weakness, and they give off their relative strength in return. The configuration shows low levels of earth and water, for example. So other individuals who have strength there are usually attracted to me ( or I attracted to them). And I have shown how my children and I complement each other, using this configuration. Also, remember what was said about souls choosing an environment- and remember that souls essentially choose parents, not the other way around.

*Note: Re: Fig. #3: Sun is 13 degrees Gemini, Venus is 7, Uranus 9, and Saturn 28. Mars is 7 degrees Leo, Pluto 8, and Jupiter 28. Complementary comparisons of the author and his children are not shown.*

In closing, let me say something further about energies, starting with my residence. When I look out back, I may see a fox, raccoon, opossum, numerous different birds- and deer. And I see a wooded, and endless horizon. And I am reminded of Jacob, Essau, Isaac, Rachel, Noah, etc. I am also reminded of that famous venison (stew). So, again, energies in one's environment may remind him of the role he is to play (or roles he has played).

There are spiritual, biological, male, female, mind, and other energies. In the Book of Matthew, for example, the biological lineage of Jesus is given. In the Book of Luke, there is the spiritual lineage. You will note that the lineage diverges during the time of Solomon, because the biological and spiritual missions diverge. It is good to be in unity of mind, body, and soul. Then, the mission will be one. And there can be unity of purpose with God.

Generally, male energy is aggressive, fiery (like the sun), and it seeks its complement, or balance (physically) in the energy of the female (which is lunar). Basically, the power of the sun and moon, together, are used to make, and keep grass green, and keep it from turning gray (brown). And that may be a key to health, vitality, and longevity.

Before I attained Unity, in 1980, I had many occasions (in visions, or dreams) when I "flirted" with uniting with the sun. When I did (fully) in the summer of 1980, it literally poured down rain, on earth in Chicago (7/20/1980). And in the vision, it rained (pleasantly), and there was soft and wonderful music. It was as if all creation rejoiced - And celebrated. (Note that I merged into the sun, but the effect, rain, is "lunar" energy- plus "mind" energy).

And I have experienced that unity, I think, one or more times since then (in visions). But, my point is this: I talked to a woman who said that she experienced unity, somewhat like I have just described, with the moon. And I thought we were all sparks of God (symbolized by the sun).

The sun and moon are opposites. The sun (or more colors) makes matter darker. Pigmentation increases. It is stored energy, within melanin. Also, as you get older, the skin darkens. The skin and hair reflect this abundance of energy in darker peoples. The absence of the sun lightens matter. The hair and eyes are lighter. The opposite holds true for light: more colors makes light lighter.

There is probably an archetype that inclines men to select a female form, and appearance, (of fertility) and capability that will perpetuate (him/her) as exemplified (in one instance) by the Miss America Pageant. So, that is a pageant of "desirable" lunar ("lighter") energy- for men. As women get older, as we noted, they get darker, and usually lose their youthful (fertile) shape. So, opposites here, show attraction; the sun seeks the moon.

A woman's search for sun energy may first involve "men of means." And it is more a search for a protected, secure, stable environment. Power, whether of intellect, wealth, strength, etc., may be seen as a means to secure that protected environment. Women have even been known to seek the "tall, dark, and handsome" (i.e., non-deformed DNA) type, which ensures "energy" for survival of the fittest, protection, etc. A lot of the interplay between men and women is to demonstrate to her, or reassure her of this caring, concern, protection.

In some Eastern cultures, differences of energy have been noted for centuries. The lunar is called yin, and the solar, yang. And the ideal sought, is balance. Anyway, men and women may be very different in some ways we are not quite aware of. If you take Bosnia, for example. Why don't the women go out and grab a bunch of men and rape them as an act of aggression and war? Genetically and biologically, they are the same as males who do, or have done this. Is that against the very nature of women? The sperm starts out by being aggressive. We need a way to bring out what is best in men and women- and also what is natural. But aggressive tendencies must be recognized (or their complement); and conduct must be channeled, or controlled in ways that are acceptable.

In sports, males like to take the "ball" to the net, the hoop, the hole, and the end zone. Usually female, cheerleaders dress, dance, and "chant" (demonstrating wonderful "feminine" attributes) to urge the males on. And in basketball, for instance, males "invade" territory (dressed appropriately) and may "score" well over 100 points to satisfy "the sport" and claim final victory.

Volley ball may be one of the more "feminine" sports, and is more readily engaged in by females. There is back and forth, back and forth (squabbles). Here, you want to prevent, or deflect being "scored upon," and keep "your territory" from being invaded. Also, you send your ball (male) out to penetrate "their" territory.

In baseball, when "at bat," you are in charge, and you may hit home runs, singles, triples, grand slams, etc. And you are expected to "swing your bat" effectively, unless you are a "medicine man, or priest" ( pitcher).

In football, you have no bat, but you throw your whole body into the process of scoring. And males are given such names as "tight end," "running back," "tail back," etc. Males sometime remind themselves that sports are only games (simulation). But, then, someone adds that they are a business (i.e., real territory, and other human needs and wants are involved). To win may be like getting offspring. To win a trophy is like getting gifted, wonderful, lovely, children who have all the attributes associated with the prize: courage, perseverance, intellect, oversight (strategy), etc.

So, it is interesting to look at the psychological, variable, and specific characteristics of sports, and its participants. Referees, for example, usually make sure things don't get too much out of control, and that some focus is maintained.

Anyway, the point is: males are territorial. This means, they naturally go to "war" to acquire, or maintain territory. Athletic games reenact this disposition. Sometimes this energy gets out of control. And that will help explain the male jail population, gangs; the Cold War, Angola, and also Bosnia.

When real males sense danger, they will "circle the wagons." And there are males and females who exemplify the fact that "girls just want to have fun."

They are more interested in parties, nails, hair, and social status. These are viewed by real males with disgust, and exasperation. For example, if real males have one of their own in captivity, they will turn that place into a desert, to get him.

Females will often comply with whatever conditions exist, because the energy is like the moon. They may fix what is in "their territory." Then, there may be complaint. But, finally, real males will be called upon to fix things "by any means necessary."

Real males will never, ever comply against their will, and if you have an evil, oppressive, and irrational system like South Africa, Northern Ireland, or the USA, either you will have an outright war, or you will fill your jails, in a nevertheless relentless, but covert war of rebellion and resistance.

The only way to begin to slow down a real male is to destroy his body. But, since he knows his soul is immortal, he will just laugh at you, and keep coming. And keep coming... and keep coming... because there is a process called Resurrection.

When you fight real males, they may become kamikaze pilots. They may become "suicide" bombers. Perhaps, we should view the "disgruntled postal employees" similarly. President Truman recognized that the only way to deal with real men (in combat) is to try to erase their memory from the universe!

So, understand: the earth must turn, and the moon must vary, and the winds must blow - to keep the relentless, pounding energy of the sun from turning its sights into a desert. And when the male energy is developed enough to "hook up with God," Goliath will surely die; and Pharaoh will certainly "let my people go!"

Many males make good soldiers because they will shut... up, and do what they're told! And they're taught to mind their own business, and to want to know what they have a need to know. If you have good, righteous leadership, that can be good. Otherwise, it is a disaster. Military males are also often taught to be logical, cool headed, and rational. And now, people are correctly being taught to use both sides of their brain. Males and females can probably profit from some military training.

Today, many males are "circling the wagons" because there are over a million males in prisons! The USA is actually bankrupt! The S&L's actually collapsed in 1988! Businesses are collapsing, yet they call it downsizing. There is a crime epidemic. People are often paid insufficient wages (because of the insane economic system). Only about 120 million of 260 million citizens work (because of the insane economic system). Legal and illegal drug use is excessive. Taxes are excessive- and increasing. And the leadership is interested in (political, and other) parties, Whitewater, Waco, hair, nails, getting reelected, and social status.

So, the leadership are like the girls who just want to have fun. And many males and females are cowards. That's probably one good reason why Bill Clinton will not be reelected – unless he changes his ways. And the congressional candidates who helped create the problems- or cannot solve them, will not be elected. Any male who does not have a real plan to solve the USA debt problem, the drug problem, the crime problem, and the gang problem, is not a real male.

But, back to comparing male and female energies. When females become unduly aggressive, dominant; and they are also selfish, dishonest, greedy, jealous, etc., dysfunction will probably follow. And so, this helps explain the purported story of Adam, Eve, and the so-called devil. That story may be the first instance of projection, in our "modern" human history.

When males have an undue amount of "lunar" energy, monsters, like John Wayne Gacy, Jeffrey Dahmer, Richard Speck, etc., are created. Then, there are monstrosities, like Jim Jones, Susan Smith, and those who toss their children out of windows. We call them *lunatics!* They're unbalanced. And the USA environment is fertile ground for these kinds of devils. So, the environment in the USA really needs to be changed.

So, how do we get better souls? You create a better environment, and you will get better souls coming into that condition.

Somehow, I sensed the possibility of a son. And I bought him some encyclopedias, beginning in about February, 1993. And though it seems a little strange, when he wants to get "books," those are the books he wants. And, it has been noticed that on the last few occasions, he likes to start looking at the same (specific) book. So, you can invite souls into an environment. You can bless them before they are even conceived-and before they are born. You can, and should ask God- and the universe, to bless a soul that will be entrusted to you. (Remember, he really belongs to himself-and God). And you can ask God for good souls. He may not give you what you want. He will undoubtedly give what you need.

You can, of course, be a better person- thereby creating a better environment, and you will get the increased possibility of a better soul. Be loving, care, share; have courage; be just, and you may get a soul to match that environment.

Here, let's take a few examples of how a soul may go shopping for parents. It is almost like going into a food store, with a certain amount of money. And you also know what you want and need.

As you know, Abraham Lincoln had a great impact on African Americans. So, God and Abraham would have known that impact was probable when he went shopping for DNA and parents. Abraham resembles Jacob and King David in some ways. Let's also assume that Abraham was *King James I*, of England.

God says, "What's up, Soul?" (Or maybe, He calls him Jimmy, etc.).

"Well, I'm getting a little bored up here. I think I'm ready for another lifetime."

"OK, you have 50 talents available to you. How do you wish to spend them?"

"I want to go down to the USA and fix that slavery mess, down there. You know how I despise oppressors- the same as you. So, I guess I could go down there and be one of them. You know my determination. Right makes might, I always say. I could lead them out of slavery, all right. No problem. I could raise an army. We could create a separate state. You remember what I did to the Philistines?"

"Well, Soul, you do have the bloodlines in place to be one of them. But I have something else in mind. There's a bloodline through the Lincolns. It's a good bloodline. We want to make you president, over the oppressors. You have a pretty good record as a king. You will get your army. We can use your iron will, to get the job done. You'll only get about a year of formal schooling. Pay close attention to what your son, Solomon (I mean, Thomas Jefferson, had to say). You guys are so similar, almost like twins. But, you were always more of a rowdy (I mean fighter). Anyway, We will guide you in all the things you need to know."

Then, God says, "Check out Thomas Lincoln, and here are some other choices. Here are the characteristics that you can choose from. You will be out in the wilderness, and on the frontier. It would be wise to select a very durable body. And you know you like to wrestle, from the time you were Jacob. So, you may want to be strong enough to be a winner. You know how you are about winning.

"And you like to write, and tell stories- from the time you were King David. We want to go easy on your looks. We don't want you too attractive. Remember Bathsheba. We don't want to make you too ugly, though. You won't get to be president by "divine rights-" as in England. The people have to choose you. You don't want to scare potential voters away by being too comely.

"You will have access to the Bible you helped commission. At times, that may be about the only book available to you. We will be in touch, because you will certainly need Us. Your name, this time, will be Abraham Lincoln! Good luck and I bless!

Abraham protests about being among the oppressors until God reminds him that he did it while in ancient Israel. He hid out among the Philistines, and pretended to be one of them. So, Abraham tells God that he will cool it. And if the situation becomes unbearable, then, he will speak out.

It is interesting to consider how Abraham would come into resurrection today. He was very proud of being a captain in the Blackhawk campaign. He invested a lot into trying to bring out the best in America, (and in people). He would be disgusted with America! He invested a lot in the African American community, too. He would probably be disgusted to learn that community does so little for itself, cares so little for each other, or does so little for each other, etc. Too many of them, and America (you guessed it): "just wannna have fun."

Now, consider another candidate for resurrection. "Ivan The Terrible" has 6 talents (of DNA). In the outcome, he will demonstrate that one can only access or employ DNA, etc., that one has a "right" to (or "legitimate" need, or desire for). Look at the broad diversity of Rose Kennedy's children as an example of this principle. He may use most on looks, size, and a life that is as easy as possible. And the situation may be very similar for "Lovely Eve."

"Oh God," she says. "My self-esteem is so low, from last time. I'm so sorry for Telling Adam, "The devil made me do it." I need some really good looks to make me feel better. You know, if Adam had paid more attention to me, instead of naming animals so much, things would have been so much better. And you know, he really should have spent more time with me. He (or somebody) will certainly notice me next time. I want that fabulous figure, there. And I'll take those stunningly good looks. And I'll take those parents there. They will be easy to manipulate. And I will usually get my way. And I can build up my self-esteem."

So, many people have not built up too many worthwhile talents. And it's just about HARVEST TIME!

But, back to our original topic: How do we heal the mind?

We heal it with unity, with truth, and with facts. Right activity, rest, and reassurance are needed. If you want to heal the mind, turn it over to God, so he can work on it. You ought to use the Christ-Link. Follow your urges to do the right thing, and get healed.

For some, it will be reassuring (to the mind) to know that Our Creator is today Retaking the earth from the devils. For, He needs it for those who choose Him. They are His chosen.

For others, it will cause great consternation.
It's like a movie that came out a few years ago. For some, it will be like a nightmare. But, it's true. We're here...! We're back...! And this time, we're not going away from pharaoh. Pharaoh is going someplace!

Also, know that pork is possibly poison- and evil. Be aware of your diet. Homosexuality is a perversion of energies, and is evil. The USA economic system is materialistic, irrational, oppressive, and satanic. Its government is too much like a useless parasite, or leech. Accepting its values is unhealthy.

To have a healthy mind, one should practice caring and sharing, which is love. One should see mind as just part of a trinity, that also includes the body and soul. Maintain your body with breathing and physical exercise. Emphasize and practice courage. Know that technology and science must be used to liberate people, not enslave them- as is now the case.

The body functions somewhat like a computer. Give it a lot of conflicting instructions: lies, half-truths; selfishness, unwarranted thoughts, feelings, concepts- and it goes "crazy"(gives irrational responses). Be good to your body.

Realize that people who don't remember any of their dreams may either have some functional inhibitor, or not be fully healthy (and in touch with their subconscious).

Finally, I will not discuss sexuality and motivation here. Suffice to say, sexuality is also an expression of the desire for unity and wholeness, in addition to perpetuation. The best expression of sexuality is between those in love, when there is caring and sharing.

*"Healing begins with the mind, and ends at One with the universe."*

    A few years ago, Whitney Houston sang a song: It said, "Where do broken hearts go? Can they find their way home, back to the open arms of a love that's waiting there? And if somebody loves you, won't they always love you? I look in your eyes, and I know that you still care, for me."

    And the song is very true. But it's not just true for broken hearts. It's not just true for broken bodies, or broken souls. It is also true for broken minds.

    And souls do find their way back, lifetime after lifetime, to lands, peoples, friends and kinsmen, to find love and familiarity again.

    And when souls really want to become healthy again, they find their way back to the open arms of God.

    And so, I say this for Our Father, and myself:

"Wholeness (and health of mind) is yours, for the asking.

Just choose justice, truth, and sharing

And you will be back home.


*"Healing begins with the mind, and ends at One with the universe."*

# 13 UPDATE – OBSERVATIONS OF NOAH

Noah is now over 18-years old. And it is now over 17-years since I wrote the *Observations of Noah* on June 25, 1995. He was then 15-months old. Noah is attending Northwestern University, and in his Freshman year.

He has been an Honors Student since grammar school. And he continued on the road of academic excellence, graduating High School in the top 1-percent of his class, with high honors.

Noah was a member of his high school's *Mathletes Math Team* and its *Scholastic Bowl*.

Outside of school, he took Taekwondo lessons and has received his Black Belt.
Noah is an ideal person in many ways, and a wonderful son. I have expressed some of my feelings about him in the following three selections: *My Delightful Son, Noah is Great*, and *Prayer-1*.

After reading the selections that reference to Noah, read the selection, *Barack Obama to Complete the Presidency of Abraham Lincoln* (below) to learn more about how the USA fits into Bible Prophecy and about the discovery-revelation that President Barack Obama is the reincarnation of Abraham Lincoln. Also read the selection, *The Solution to Our Economic and Social Future: Jubilee and Other Remedies* to get a better understanding of where we are in time, and where the country (and world) is headed.

# 14 MY DELIGHTFUL SUN

Noah is my delightful son.

He is my delightful sun.

He's my fire, earth air, and water.

Noah is my delightful son.

## 15 NOAH IS GREAT

He's patient w/me:

Kind,

Generous,

Compassionate,

Considerate, loving,

Forgiving,

Sympathetic,

Warm-hearted,

Long-suffering,

Smart,

Intelligent,

Thoughtful,

Creative,

Idealistic,

Fun-loving,

Dare-devilish,

Hard-working,

Patient w/me,

& great!

# 16 PRAYER – I

Our Father, Who is in Heaven,
Holy is Your Name.

*Your Kingdom be strengthened* in Noah, #
In the earth, among your Chosen,
In the 144, 000,

In Barack and Michelle Obama,
Sasha and Malia,*
Tonya and Runako, # Chicagoland,
And the United States of America
*As it is in Heaven.*

Give us this day
Our daily bread
And forgive us our debts,
As we forgive our debtors.

Lead us not into temptation,
But deliver us from all evil,

For yours is the Kingdom
Of the Heavens
And the earth,
And the Power,
And the Glory,
Forever, and ever.

Amen. (OM)

*Members of the Obama Family

#Members of the Khalim (Robinson) Family

# 17 UPDATE – OBSERVATIONS OF THE AUTHOR

On 5/2/2000, I had the following experience during the period I was writing *The Resurrection of Noah*. That book is about "how life works," how the birth and death of souls works, and what the "Bibles" say about reincarnation. Based on many verses in the Qur'an and the Bible, I had a suspicion that the Prophet Muhammad may be the reincarnation of Moses. I planned a meditation session, (a "conscious," though immobile state) to research the matter. And I carefully formulated the question that I wanted to ask. I successfully went into meditation. And this is what I saw:

First, there were the sights and sounds of mighty, swirling winds, and sand, in the desert. Then, the sands morphed into a face!

"Is Prophet Muhammad the reincarnation of Moses?" I asked. The winds stopped

swirling, and the sands stood still.

"Of course," it said. And I was amazed!

Earlier, on August 4, 1999, I was in the process of writing explanations about how reincarnation works in that same book. At about 10:30 pm, I was lying in bed and I thought: Wouldn't it be cool if I could write a story on any of my (supposed) incarnations, or others where I was "famous" – and sell it.

I had this experience: My "consciousness" went back to 1955, and then to Jefferson Elementary School, the first school I attended in Chicago. I wondered what this meant. I started researching Thomas Jefferson, on the Internet, and in my home Encyclopedias. Amazingly, at about 1:54 AM, I received an email from a guy named Jefferson (Jefrsn@aol.com) *while I was researching Jefferson.* I told Jefferson about this synchronicity. I told him about my question, and about my quest. Finally, I wrote an email to Jeannette DeLangis, a "Psychic Hostess," on AOL, asking her the same question, "Am I the Reincarnation of Thomas Jefferson?"

On August 5, 1999, at about 11:46 AM, I went into meditation. I asked, "Am I the Reincarnation of Thomas Jefferson?"

A display "window" appeared. The "Yes" response (answer) was clicked.

On 2/23/2002, I discovered that Thomas Jefferson is/was the reincarnation of Jacob.

"Was Thomas Jefferson the reincarnation of Jacob, father of the 12 boys who became known as the Nation of Israel?" The display "window" appeared. The "Yes" response (answer) was clicked.

On about June 21, 2008, I had a dream indicating that President Barack Obama is the reincarnation of Abraham Lincoln. Since that time I have watched Mr. Obama closely, and I am about 80% - 100% certain that Barack Obama is the same soul as Abraham Lincoln. He seems to often ask himself, "What would Lincoln do? What did Lincoln do?" And he has been known to "retrace and duplicate" Lincoln's known travels, routes, itineraries, ways of thinking, and ways of doing things. See the selection, *Barack Obama to Complete the Presidency of Abraham Lincoln*, at the end of this Epilogue to see how I have incorporated this knowledge-information about Lincoln-Obama into my overall message.

**Birth:**

Just moments after my umbilical cord was cut, I raised my head up high and looked all around the room. Side-to-side, I looked - all around the room! I lowered myself back down. Then, I did it again! The people in the room were astonished!

**Background:**

I spent the first 11 years of my life in Mississippi. Then, my family and I moved to Chicago, where I attended, first, Thomas Jefferson Elementary School, and lastly, DeVry University.

Though I was born into a Christian family, at about the age of 14, I began the study all major religions, including Christianity, Judaism, Islam, Buddhism, Shinto, and Hinduism. At about the age of 20, I embraced Islam. At the age of 27, I began the practice of Yoga and Kabala. And on July 20, 1980, I obtained Unity.

Almost immediately after practicing Yoga and Kabala, I was able to "see" on the other side, in visions, dreams, and during Astral travels. In the autobiography, *The Second Coming*, I tell you about what I saw, and what it means. I also tell, in some detail, about my quest, research, and experiences.

The "Bibles" indicate that the Christian *"Second Coming"* started during the Clinton administration. These times complete the cycle starting with "Adam," and during these times, God begins to fully re- establish His sovereignty over the earth.

It is a time when science, technology, and innovation create the conditions for "heaven on earth," and when those conditions and individuals in opposition to truth, justice, caring, sharing, openness, and privacy will not exist on earth.

*The Second Coming* (this era) has enormous implications for the political, military, economic, and social history of the USA - and for the future of the world. We must strive to provide useful information and a hopeful ideology as part of an evolving blueprint for action, and the establishment of the real New World Order.

# 18 UPDATE: OBSERVATIONS OF SUSAN

My observation is that not much has changed of significance and/or qualitatively in Susan's life. It does seem that she has mellowed-out, settled down, and become non-combative and non-confrontational compared to where she was about 15-years ago.

# 19 BARACK OBAMA TO COMPLETE THE PRESIDENCY OF ABRAHAM LINCOLN

An Example: How Life Really Works on Earth

My father is God.

He rules the whole universe. And to accent that point, my natural father's name is Samuel, which means, "His name is God."

My Mom is Mother Earth: very special, and indispensable to life on earth.

And to accentuate points in my past and present, my natural Mom is known as Ruby: a prize, a gem, and very precious.

My Mom and Dad brought me into this world, and they educate and nurture me. Mom feeds me all her delicious fruits: pears, peaches, melons, bananas, and grapes. She gives me nutritious and delicious foods to eat. She gives me air to breathe.

Early in the morning, Mom feeds me coffee: (caffeine). And this is the only drug I need – all day long.

I love to observe my Mother's air, and windy breezes, her rain and thunderstorms.

I love my Mother's silence.

My Mom is very beautiful; her skies are gorgeous. Her mountains leave me breathless!

Today, I was watching my Mom briskly swing the maple tree branches back-and-forth on the tree across the street from my house. I delight in seeing Mom do her thing.

Once Mom and Dad took me high above the earth, and I looked down on the West/North central portion of the USA.

And once again they lifted me up so I could look down upon central, southern, west-central Africa.

Once they took me up so high that I saw a whole galaxy slowly rotating. How about that?

Mom and Dad lifted me up and allowed me to fly (merge) into the sun, several times. The first time, the merging was blissful and loving: like I was in heaven. After the merging, there was light, orchestra-like music. And then it rained softly. I do not remember music and rain in the subsequent mergings.

Mom and Dad showed me myself as a soldier in Japan, in 1637, when we expelled the Christians. I was possibly torn between the loyalties of my native religion and Christianity, and my loyalty to the State.

And in China, they showed me why I'm interested in Martial Arts. I could throw a board right through the chest of a man. And I did.

Mom and Dad let me "see" and "listen" to Moses. He was very soft spoken. Not sure his appearance was what I expected. Moses looked a lot like Isaac Hayes.

They let me look-in on Prophet Muhammad once: interesting family marital situation. I was wondering how he managed.

Once they showed me Solomon. He was not only handsome. Solomon was a "beautiful," manly man.

I incarnated into the regions and the peoples, from Japan to England, and from Africa to America. So, all peoples of the world are part of me. And I am part and parcel of them.

The following is what I have to tell you; stuff that my Mom and Dad showed me. Following that, I will tell you, why now?

1. Thomas Jefferson is the reincarnation of Jacob, father of *the* renowned 12-boys that became known as Israel.
2. Prophet Muhammad is the reincarnation of Moses. This *is* no joke, and it was presented to me as an almost obvious fact.
3. President Barack Obama is the reincarnation of President Abraham Lincoln.
4. I was born "Jimmie." But I changed my name to James, which is a variation of Jimmy (Jimmie): Jacob, because I am he.
5. Since Moses is *my* "son," and Prophet Muhammad *is* Moses – the same soul (and therefore obviously my "son"), how cool is that?
6. Since Jesus traces his lineage through *my* 12-boys, he is also my "son."
7. I have hesitated to tell you about some of the reincarnations. Some of it sounds self-serving, or narcissistic, or whatever. It sounds strange to me too.

**The scriptures explain reincarnation, and how life works thusly:**

Luke 20:38 says, **"For He (God) is not a God of the dead, but of the living: for all live in Him."**

Matthew 22:31,32 says, **"But as touching the resurrection of the dead, have ye not read that which was spoken unto you by God, saying, I am the God of Abraham, and the God of Isaac, and the God of Jacob? God is not the God of the dead, but of the living."**

Matthew 9:23, says, **"And when Jesus came into the ruler's house, and saw the minstrel and the people making a noise,**

24) **He said unto them, Give place: for the maid is not dead, but sleepeth. And they laughed him to scorn.**

**25) But when the people were put forth, he went in, and took her by the hand, and the maid arose.**

In Chapter 39:42, the Holy Qur'an says, **"It is Allah Who takes away the souls at the time of their death, and those that die not, during their sleep. He keeps those souls for which He has ordained death and sends the rest back for a term appointed...."**

In Chapter 2:28, it says, **How can you disbelieve in Allah? Seeing that you were dead and He gave you life. Then He will give you death, then again will bring you to life, and then unto Him you will return."**

Now, the USA is very special, in positive, and in negative ways. *It is Israel*; and it is an amalgam of empires Greece/Rome. Look at the sophistry, greed, evil, decadence, and the hatefulness in its politics, and in its economics; and you can immediately see what I mean.

Look at its militarism.

Look at the good. That is all around us, but sometimes it exists by a few frayed threads.

The USA is leader of the $7^{th}$, $8^{th}$ (and last) world Power, according to the Torah and the Gospels.

What comes next is described in the Torah, Gospels, and Qur'an as a golden age of peace, prosperity, accountability, brotherhood, and all that kind of stuff.

It says that Satan will be bound 1000-years. But, back to now:

President Obama is finishing up his interrupted presidency as Abraham Lincoln. He is a national treasure, and must be protected at all costs.

The whole economic, social, and world order will change. When they try to put a price and a monetary value on everything, they inevitably put the wrong price on just about everything.

They try to maximize their profits, with little regard for people. They have global greed, without global regulation and accountability, and monitoring. No wonder, *"Things Fall Apart."* (See sunracommunications.com: *The Resurrection of Noah, The Second Coming*, et.al.)

**Solutions**: **Since the USA is the *real* Israel,** we can build a Second Solomon Temple right here is Illinois – where ***water*** *is* plentiful, *and the land is truly flowing "with milk and honey."*

We can recombine my son's two major religions, Judaism and Islam back into one faith – with Christianity and Science (and common sense) added in.

Let us be temperate, moderate, and cautious in making the necessary changes.

Don't allow trigger-happy nations continue to instigate, start, and conduct these periodic, dangerous wars!

Do not allow nuclear annihilation. Respect and protect my Mom.

*Why now?* I realized this a few days ago: My time for completing my mission is rapidly coming to a close. I *have to* act now!

Mom and Dad are watching.

# 20 THE SOLUTION TO OUR ECONOMIC AND SOCIAL FUTURE: JUBILEE AND OTHER REMEDIES

The current economic and social models do not/will not work in our global economy. The reasons are obvious.

Situations/Conditions:

- Manufacturers, service providers, employers, and commodity markets seek out the cheapest labor and the lowest price possible as an expense; the opposite is true when they are marketing (selling) their product. And the current practices of outsourcing and moving manufacturing jobs overseas results in "a race to the bottom."

- Workers, goods, and services are increasingly priced out of the market in the "Developed World." And to mollify them, consumers have access to "cheap" imported manufactured goods.

- What used to be a local or national economy (and manageable) is now hoisted onto the world stage, part of a mammoth enterprise, that global community.

- When employers attempt to adjust to reduced demand, they lay off workers, cut production and operations. They create a catch-22, a snowball effect, an economy spiraling downward. There is a reduced demand for products and services, and overall spending is reduced. Succeeding and preceding industry related employers lay off workers in response to a reduced demand for their products and services, ad infinitum. The herd mentality takes over. The loss of jobs creates greater loss of jobs. This is a self-inflicted destruction of economies: local, national, and international. Thus, The Great Recession of 2007 was created.

- When you put a price on almost everything, and the price keeps creeping up and up, over time almost everything becomes too costly for too many. Look at the pricing and cost of housing or automobiles in the USA as examples.

- The reason you cannot put the *right* price on specific products, goods, and services is that items invariably do not reflect various costs, benefits, or losses. For example, if a factory moves to China and then ships its products back to the USA, the cost of the imported products sold in USA stores do not reflect the social, moral, and environmental costs associated with the loss of jobs, increased trade deficits, and social and economic loss and disruption in USA communities, etc.

- When you put a price (monetary value) on almost everything, you inevitably put the wrong price on almost everything: See the excerpt from the article below by Douglas McIntyre as an example of how this society *prices* the value of labor and jobs.

Is one CEO worth the price of many, many workers as is indicated below?

How Many Workers Can You Hire for the Price of One CEO?

By DOUGLAS MCINTYRE

See full article from Daily Finance: http://srph.it/bxw0Og

"To get a sense of how the CEO of a company you regularly do business with pays his or her employees compared to themselves, we've broken it down for you below:

**CVS Caremark** (CVS)
Thomas M. Ryan: $30.4 million (2009 Compensation) Starting Cashier:
$8/hour, $20,800/year
One CEO = 1,461 entry-level employees

**AT&T** (T)
Randall Stephenson: $29.2 million (2009 Compensation) Starting Sales Associate: $10/hour, $26,000/year
One CEO = 1,123 entry-level employees

**The Walt Disney Co.** (DIS)
Robert Iger: $29 million (2009 Compensation) Disneyland Hotel Housekeeper: $10/hour, $26,000/year One CEO = 1,115 entry-level employees

**McDonald's** (MCD)
James A. Skinner: $17.6 million (2009 Compensation) Starting Cashier: $7.25/hour, $18,850/year
One CEO = 933 entry-level employees

**Target** (TGT)
Gregg W. Steinhafel: $16.1 million (2009 Compensation) Starting Cashier: $8.50/hour, $22,100/year
One CEO = 728 entry-level employees

**Cablevision** (CVC)
Founder and Chairman Charles F. Dolan: $15 million (2009 Compensation) James L. Dolan: $17 million (2009 Compensation) Customer Service Representative: $13/hour, $33,800/year One CEO = 505 entry-level employees

**Starbucks** (SBUX)
Founder Howard Schultz: $9.9 million (2009 Compensation) Entry-level Barista: $9/hour, $23,400/year
One CEO = 423 entry-level employees

**Wal-Mart Stores** (WMT)
Michael T. Duke: $8.5 million (2009 Compensation) Starting Sales Associate: $9.75/hour, $25,350/year One CEO = 335 entry-level employees

**Nike** (NKE)
Mark G. Parker: $7.3 million (2009 Compensation)
Starting Sales Associate, NYC Store: $9/hour, $23,400/year
One CEO = 311 entry-level employees

**Time Warner Cable** (TWC)
Glenn A. Britt $15.9 million (2009 Compensation) Cable Installer: $20/hour, $52,000/year
One CEO = 305 employees

**AMR** (American Airlines, Inc.) (AMR)
Gerard J. Arpey: $5.6 million (2009 Compensation)
Entry-level Flight Attendant, flying minimum domestic hours: $20.24/hour, $21,252/year
One CEO = 263 entry-level employees

**FedEx** (FDX)
Founder Frederick W. Smith: $8.48 million (2009 compensation) Handler: $13/hour, $33,800/year
One CEO = 251 entry-level employees

**Costco** (COST)
James D. Sinegal: $2.3 million (2009 Compensation) Starting Sales Associate: $11/hour, $28,600/year One CEO = 115 entry-level employees

**JPMorgan Chase & Co.** (JPM)
James Dimon: $1.3 million (2009 Compensation) Bank teller: $12/hour, $31,200/year
One CEO = 41 entry-level employees"

- Bill Gates and Warren Buffett made so much money that they recently got together and came up with processes, methods, and vehicles to effectively *give* some of it away.

Usury:

　Regarding Usury:

　　Our righteous forbears forbade usury, (excessive interest), and interest (excessive or not) is part of what pushes the price of everything up and up.

Solutions:

- Today's economy requires timed-coordination, and thoughtful, sequenced actions. The global economy must be viewed as **one** organism; the goal must be to get the goods and services to the people – not put a "price" on everything, which inevitably disables the whole world economy. We cannot put the right price on goods and services in our own region. Not in our own country. It is the Mother of Economic Folly to play "the game of pricing" worldwide, vying for a price, labor, health care advantage here, or some other advantage there.

- What if 1000 or 100,000 employers decided *simultaneously* to hire 1, 2, or 3 employees, just as *they effectively* (consciously or unconsciously) decided to lay off 1, 2, 3, or more employees? (i.e., Why not do the reverse of what created the Great Recession of 2007?)

- We need to look at how today's successful economies operate, and consider emulating or simulating their prototypes in some morally and ethically acceptable manner. How can we simulate or emulate some things that China, India, Brazil, and others do?

- An enterprise can compensate for unaffordable costs by getting volunteer (free) labor, getting the workers to lower their wages, by eliminating or reducing health care costs, inventory costs, utility costs, etc. The enterprise can seek to effectively reduce costs by being more productive. Note: There are "armies" of the unemployed and underemployed waiting to be enlisted as "volunteers."

- We can lower the price of everything, and put almost everything within reach of almost everyone.

- Just like a company passes cost increases along to its customers, with "free" and/or reduced labor and health care costs, it can pass the *decreased* costs along.

- Everyone can participate in the economy; everyone can share in the work, and in the fruits of their labor.

- Consider, if everything could be gotten "free," everything could be *given* "free." Charities routinely operate in a fashion similar to this. The emphasis then is on the good or service, not the "price."

- Effectively, our aim should be to take the "price" off many goods and services, and make the production, provisioning, and distribution of the benefit our objective.

A. The Solution is "Jubilee" and the Implementation of "Christian" Values

Remember?

"The earth is the LORD'S, and the fullness thereof; the world, and they that dwell therein." (Psalms 24:1.)

"...Freely, you have received, freely you must give." (Matthew 10:8.) "And all that believed were together, and had all things common; and sold their possessions and goods, and parted them to all men, as every man had need." (Acts 2:44-45.)

"And the multitude of them that believed were of one heart and of one soul: neither said any of them that ought of the things which he possessed was his own; but they had all things common. And with great power gave the apostles witness of the resurrection of the Lord Jesus: and great grace was upon them all. Neither was there any among them that lacked: for as many as were possessors of lands or houses sold them, and brought the prices of the things that were sold, And laid them down at the apostles' feet: and distribution was made unto every man according as he had need." (Acts 4:32-35.)

Jubilee:

If I owe you $500, and you owe me $500, we don't owe each other *anything*. How is it that 99% of governments (at all levels) and individuals, etc. are indebted?

The USA National Debt is now over $16 Trillion

Consider how the USA national debt increased from the time of President Jimmy Carter: a) It was about $994 billion when Jimmy Carter left office; b) It was about $2.867 trillion when Ronald Reagan left office; c) It was about $4.351 trillion when H.W. Bush left office; d) It was about $5.638 trillion when Bill Clinton left office; e) It was about $10.7 trillion in December, 2008 (when the economy was near the beginning of its recent downward spiral); f) It is over $15 trillion today, in part due to two wars, drug benefits, and tax cuts.

Many governments are flirting with economic disaster at the national, state, and local levels. This is also true with respect to individuals, businesses, etc. Therefore, the Lord our God has made provision for all in the *Law of Jubilee*:

"And thou shall number 7 Sabbaths of years unto thee, 7 times 7 years; and the space of 7 Sabbaths of years shall be unto thee 40 and 9 years. Then shalt thou cause the trumpet of the Jubilee to sound on the 10th day of the 7th month, in the Day of Atonement shall ye make the trumpet sound throughout the land. And ye shall hallow the fiftieth year, and proclaim liberty throughout all the land unto all the inhabitants thereof: it shall be a Jubilee unto you. And ye shall return every man unto his possessions, and ye shall return every man unto his family." (Leviticus 25:8-13.)

"Jubilee will cancel (reset to zero or make current) all debt, including federal (national), state, local, business, farm, individual, student, family, and international. So, all countries, like the USA, Russia, Greece, Poland, Mexico, Nigeria, Brazil, Zaire, Canada, etc. become completely free of debt." ***Jubilee could be implemented over a period of 5-years, and does not have to be completed all at once.***

B. Jobs and Society: Use the Civilian Conservation Corps (CCC) and Works Progress Administration (WPA) of *The New Deal* as Models

We could set up (or use existing) government and/or private corporations, or Community Councils, at the local, county, state, and national levels to engage, employ, educate, train, and enlist our youth, adults, and elders in transforming the culture, lives, and communities of our nation for the $21^{st}$ Century.

Beginning at the local level, these facilities will serve every city block, and every community, as necessary.

- The Local Community Council will be organized to employ, enlist, educate, rehabilitate, train, and assimilate preschoolers, those 5-65 years old, etc., grouped appropriately and as necessary. Payments will be made directly to participants.

- This acculturation and training will be administered by qualified elders, teachers, scholars, and ministers.

- The local, county, state, and national councils' work will cut off the supply of recruits to the gangs, and when fully implemented (with other efforts) will cut off the supply of, and/or minimize the use of illegal drugs. Note: Street gangs are a threat to the safety and security of the society and the state.

- This system of cutting off the supply of recruits can also be modified, tailored, and used to cut off the supply of recruits to the Taliban and Al-Qaeda. For reference, see how a variation of this general idea was implemented in ancient Sparta; here, children were recruited to be useful and productive members (soldiers, warriors) of the society. Consider the Boy Scouts as a template.

- The Community Councils can be organized along military models, (i.e., Private, Corporal, Sergeant, Staff Sergeant, Lieutenant, Captain, Major, Lieutenant Colonel, Colonel, Brigadier General, etc., or persons having comparable or equivalent Civil Service rank.

C. Precedents: For What Must be Done

1. The Emancipation Proclamation

2. The Louisiana Purchase

3. The colonization/acquisition of the United States

4. Reparations payments to the state of Israel

5. Reparations payments to Japanese Americans who were wrongfully incarcerated in the USA

6. Infrastructure, employment, and construction programs (of the CCC and the WPA) under President Franklin D. Roosevelt

Consider the Amish as a Possible (Partial) Template

Retirement

"When the Amish choose to retire is neither a set nor fixed time. Considerations of the person's health, the family's needs, and personal desires all play an important part in determining when retirement may occur, usually between the ages of fifty to seventy. The elderly do not go to a retirement facility; they remain at home. If the family house is large enough they continue living with everyone else. Oftentimes there is an adjacent dwelling, called the Grossdaadi Haus, where grandparents take up residence. Retired people continue to help with work on the farm and within the home, working at their own pace as they are able. This allows them independence but does not strip them of family involvement.

"The Amish method of retirement ensures that the elderly maintain contact with family and relatives. Loneliness is not a problem because they keep meaningful social contacts through various community events, such as frolics, auctions, weddings, holiday, and other community activities.

If the aged become ill or infirm, then the other family members take up caring for them. The elderly parents once helped raise the younger members, therefore the younger family care for them in their old age."

D. The Solution to Helping to Curb Terrorism Lies Within Religious and Spiritual Truths

The sage(s) say that Prophet Muhammad is the reincarnation of Moses. And Thomas Jefferson is the reincarnation of Jacob (the father of the 12 boys whose descendants became known as Israel). The fact that Prophet Muhammad is the same soul as Moses creates an opportunity to psychologically, politically, religiously, and militarily disarm some terrorist elements.

There is no fundamental difference between the USA and its fellow brothers-in-the-faith. In fact, Prophet Muhammad rightfully considered himself a guardian of Judaism and Christianity as indicated in this verse from the Qur'an:

5:48 And **We have revealed to thee the Book with the truth, verifying that which is before it of the Book and a guardian over it,** so judge between them by what Allah has revealed, and follow not their low desires, turning away from the truth that has come to thee. For every one of you We appointed a law and a way. And if Allah had pleased He would have made you a single people, but that He might try you in what He gave you. So vie one with another in virtuous deeds. To Allah you will all return, so He will inform you of that wherein you differed;

*Note: We are often reminded in the Qur'an that individuals are only responsible for their own deeds and thoughts. Why would Muhammad be guardian over the Torah and Gospel? The ... logical answer is that Muhammad (as Moses) helped reveal the Torah, and though not physically present, helped with the ministry of Jesus.*

E. Thomas Jefferson and the USA:

The fact that Thomas Jefferson is the reincarnation of Jacob (and that the USA is the closest thing we have to "Israel,") is in part reflected in the fact that the first 42-presidents of the USA are a kind of reflection and pattern of the 42-kings (individuals) listed in the books of Matthew and Luke. See the list in the following selection from *Svetlana, Angel of Love*:

1. Abraham, Gen. 11:26  Like  George Washington, 1789

2. Isaac, Gen. 21:2  Like  John Adams, 1797

3. Jacob (Israel), Gen. 25:26  Is  Thomas Jefferson, 1801

4. Judas, Gen. 29:35  Like  James Madison, 1809

5. Phares, Gen. 46:12  Like  James Monroe, 1817

6. Esrom, Gen. 46:12  Like  John Quincy Adams, 1825

7. Aram, Ruth 4:19  Like  Andrew Jackson, 1829

8. Aminadab, Num. 1:7  Like  Martin Van Buren, 1837

9. Nasson, Num. 1:7  Like  William I. Harrison, 1841

10. Salmon, Ruth 4:20  Like  John Tyler, 1841

11. Booz, Ruth 4:21  Like  James K. Polk 1845

12. Obed, Ruth 4:17  Like  Zachary Taylor, 1849

13. Jesse, Ruth 4:22  Like  Millard Fillmore, 1850

14. David, 1 Chron. 2:15  Like  Franklin Pierce, 1853

15. Solomon, 2 Samuel 12:24  Like  James Buchanan, 1857

16. Roboam, 1 Kings 11:43  Like  Abraham Lincoln, 1861

17. Abia, 1 Kings 15:1  Like  Andrew Johnson, 1865

18. Asa, 1 Kings 15:9  Like  Ulysses S. Grant, 1869

19. Josaphat, 22:41  Like  Rutherford B. Hayes, 1877

20. Joram, 2 Kings 8:16  Like  James A. Garfield, 1881

21. Ozias, 2 Kings 8:25  Like  Chester A. Arthur 1881

22. Joatham, 2 Kings 15:32  Like  Grover Cleveland, 1885

23. Achaz, 2 Kings 16:1  Like  Benjamin Harrison 1889

24. Ezekias, 2 Kings 18:1  Like  Grover Cleveland, 1890

25. Manasses, 2 Kings 21:1  Like  William McKinley, 1897

26. Amon, 2 Kings 21:18  Like  Theodore Roosevelt, 1901

27. Josias, 2 Kings 21:24  Like  William H. Taft, 1909

28. Jechonias 1 Chron. 3:16  Like  Woodrow Wilson, 1913

29. Salathiel, 1 Chron. 3:17  Like  Warren G. Harding, 1921

30. Zorobabel, 1 Chron. 3:19  Like  Calvin Coolidge, 1923

31. Abiud, (Matthew)  Like  Herbert C. Hoover, 1929

32. Eliakim, (Matthew)  Like  F. D. Roosevelt, 1933

33. Azor, (Matthew)  Like  Harry S. Truman, 1945

34. Sadoc, (Matthew)  Like  Dwight D. Eisenhower, 1953

35. Achim, (Matthew)  Like  John F. Kennedy, 1961

36. Elind, (Matthew)  Like  Lyndon B. Johnson, 1963

37. Eleazar, (Matthew) Like Richard M. Nixon, 1969

38. Matthan, (Matthew) Like Gerald R. Ford, 1974

39. Jacob, (Matthew) Like Jimmy Carter, 1977

40. Joseph, (Jesus' father) Like Ronald Wilson Reagan, 1981

41. Jesus, (Matthew) Like George H. W. Bush, 1989

42. Christ, (Matthew) Like William J. Clinton, 1993

43. None; Dispensation over. George W. Bush, 2001

44. None; New Dispensation. Barack H. Obama, 2009

Very often the comparisons show the similar, or very opposite. Some of the comparisons are listed below:

1. Abraham, and George Washington moved away from their nations and started new nations. Washington was a warrior; Abraham fought against Chedorlaomer (Gen.14:5).

3. Jacob (Israel) is the father, through his offspring, of the Hebrew nation and the West. Jefferson is the father of the ideals of the USA.

14. Franklin Pierce became the youngest President of his time. He hastened the Civil War by signing the Kansas-Nebraska Act of 1854. David was a young warrior, and the best in his character was the opposite of Pierce's.

15. Solomon was wise, and had about 1000 "wives." James Buchanan is considered one of the worst presidents because of his lack of judgment and moral courage, and the only bachelor President.

16. Abraham Lincoln saved the Union and is considered a moral individual. His counterpart, Roboam, presided over the breakup of the Jewish State into Judah, and Israel. Roboam was immoral.

28. Woodrow Wilson was a good man. His counterpart, Jechonias was a scoundrel.

30. Calvin Coolidge said the business of America is business. Salathiel, the counterpart said the business of Israel was justice and righteousness.

39. Jacob, of course is another word which means James, Jimmy, Israel; and it means "he who would provide service to his fellow man." So, Jimmy Carter works for "Habitat," an organization that provides services from man, to his fellow man.

40. Joseph (Jesus' "father") helped to prepare a channel that became the hope of humanity. The World is forever indebted to him. He went to Egypt to avoid death to his son. The counterpart, Ronald Reagan, presided over the USA becoming the world's biggest debtor nation. Also, the national debt went from about $1 trillion to 3 trillion. Reagan invaded tiny Grenada, and bullied other small nations. He also said things that had little or no resemblance to facts. Many USA citizens just loved Reagan!

41-42. Jesus was oppressed and escaped to Egypt to save his young life. As the Christ, he made a way for many, to save many lives...

| | |
|---|---|
| To tell the truth, | To be of service |
| To heal the sick | To feed the hungry |

To give man hope     To lift the oppressed

To free the captives    To comfort the weary

To encourage those who fight against evil

To lead man back to his final destination!

    Bush, the counterpart, invaded Panama. He killed the children, and women, and men in his way. He murdered tens of thousands of children, women, and men in Iraq. The USA citizens loved it. Jesus the oppressed, Bush, the oppressor! Opposites!

    During the time of Bill Clinton, the price of oil declined to about $10-11 per barrel. Surpluses appeared in the Federal Budget. The Internet and The Dot-Com bubble appeared. And some thought that the Clinton era prosperity signaled the end of regular economic cycles. And this reminds us of Jesus feeding the multitude of 5 thousand men, plus women and children, with 5 loaves and 2 fishes, and taking up, after everyone had eaten, 12 baskets full of fragments, that remained. (Matt. 14: 17-21). And the 4-thousand men, plus women and children, fed with 7 loaves, and "a few little fishes." "And they took up of the broken meat that was left 7 baskets full." (Matt. 15: 34-38).

    After Jesus left the scene, and after Steven was stoned, in 34 AD, the Covenant with Ancient Israel ended. And the dispensation (mission, torch) was given, in-turn to the Christians, and then to the Muslims.

And after Clinton, the Covenant with America ended, So, The Supreme Court selected the next president, George W. Bush.

F. Words for Posterity (From My Mom and Others): Building Culture and Values

1. The purpose of life is for maintenance, growth and development.

2. Remember, an empty wagon makes the loudest noise.

3. The number of people and the number of times that a person can be in love is limitless; because just as the universe is limitless, so is love.

4. Great people talk about ideas; small people talk about people (Tobias S. Gibson).

5. Associate with people who represent the ideals of intellect, morals, and activity (conduct). Eschew and avoid the loud, ignorant, aggressive, and disrespectful ones.

6. If you don't have anything positive and constructive to say, don't say anything; try to think before you speak. Think while you are speaking.

7. All work is honorable if you are an honorable person.

8. Take time to reflect, examine and know yourself, and remove obstacles (people and things) from your life if you want to lead a purposeful and constructive life. Remove that albatross from around your neck!

9. You will often find positive or negative characteristics lumped together in one individual: ungrateful, selfish, greedy, dishonest, and myopic qualities blind the individual, and he or she is a lost soul. The opposite is true for the honest, considerate, and humane.

# 21 INDEX

1. Ali, Muhammad; God is like the jab of, 22

2. Allah; It is Allah who takes away the souls at the time of their death, and those that die not, during their sleep. How can you disbelieve in Allah? Seeing that you were dead and He gave you life. Then He will give you death, and then again will bring you to life, and then unto Him you will return, 73. And We have revealed to thee the Book with the truth, verifying that which is before it of the Book and a guardian over it, so judge between them by what Allah has revealed, 88.

3. Chicago Bears, the; God is like the Quarterback and the *front four* of the 1985, Chicago Bears, 21.

4. Dreams; two specific dreams indicate that possibility (of Noah being gifted), a list of 17 dreams, 3; the materialist psychologists, and their fellow travelers don't understand dreams, visions, time, space, God, etc., 18; We believe that dreams and/or visions can be "normal" and useful; *We believe in the dreams of Jacob, in the dreams of Joseph,* 21; Introduction to Dreams and Visions, Dreams reflect past or future conditions, 26; the author has practiced a variation of yoga, since 1971, and this has affected the quality (clarity) of his dreams, and/or visions, 27; Do Dreams Reflect Any Reality? 37; Introduction to Dreams and Visions, 39; The Dreams and Visions, 41; Before I attained Unity, in 1980, I had many occasions (in visions, or dreams) when I "flirted" with uniting with the sun, 53; people who don't remember any of their dreams, 60; Almost immediately after practicing Yoga and Kabala, I was able to "see" on the other side, in visions, dreams, and during Astral travels, 67.

5. Energy Level; My energy level decreased and the vision wound down, 44.

6. God; He says a healthy mind should know the first reality- a higher force in the universe, which we refer to as God, 3; The presence of certain kinds, or levels of "intelligence" may actually interfere with the usage of the God-link (which we call Christ) because *choices* made by that individual are in opposition to the "Christ" principles (of sharing, caring, justice, courage). An example of this may be the sociopath, the psychopathic personality, cowards, the selfish, etc., 25; **the first** *thing that they must learn is that people are all children of God, and they will often do whatever it takes to affect a certain outcome,* Dreams and visions are a reminder that we are all like our Father, God, 26; Time, Space, and God; And we must approach the study of God's creations with proper respect-which is not the case now; I believe people with Unity can often use skill beyond the intellect, or what we call insight, or intuition (in a conscious, or dream state). It seems to be a more direct interaction with what we call the Christ-link. And, when it is the higher mind, it is the truth-or God. It will make perfect sense. It will be rational, logical, just, beautiful, and obvious. So, we should locate, and make maximum use of people who have these qualities, 27; I held him and got down on my knees and prayed for God to help him, 38; Do not go on a guilt trip like the silly pseudo-Christians, and call God's creation negative things. And know that Islam can be used with Christianity to give a balanced presentation on many matters. We are indeed back, because God is today reclaiming the earth from the devils. They were allowed a certain period of rule. THEIR SYSTEM HAS BEEN WEIGHED IN THE BALANCE, AND FOUND WANTING. THEIR TIME IS UP! 40; About 9/6/93. I was traveling over an area similar to the "Grand Canyon." I felt the kind of love that emanates from God during the experience. It is superior to anything or anyone that we know of. It makes everything, and everyone else seem subordinate to that power/feeling, purity, divinity, righteousness, 43; When I first noticed these correspondences, I thought that they would help prove that God exists because they seem to be an

indication that we are usually where we are supposed to be in our evolution- or even our address. And the order seen here indicates that Intelligence, structure, reliability, and even balance prevails in God's universe. Wherever, we are, we could possibly belong there, 50; There are spiritual, biological, male, female, mind, and other energies. In the Book of Matthew, for example, the biological lineage of Jesus is given. In the Book of Luke, there is the spiritual lineage. You will note that the lineage diverges during the time of Solomon, because the biological and spiritual missions diverge. It is good to be in unity of mind, body, and soul. Then, the mission will be one. And there can be unity of purpose with God, 53; So, understand: the earth must turn, and the moon must vary, and the winds must blow to keep the relentless, pounding energy of the sun from turning its sights into a desert. And when the male energy is developed enough to "hook up with God," Goliath will surely die; and Pharaoh will certainly "let my people go!" 55; And when souls really want to become healthy again, they find their way back to the open arms of God, 60; The "Bibles" indicate that the Christian *"Second Coming"* started during the Clinton administration. These times complete the cycle starting with "Adam," and during these times, God begins to fully re-establish His sovereignty over the earth, 67; For He (God) is not a God of the dead, but of the living: for all live in Him, 72; Therefore, the Lord our God has made provision for all in the

*Law of Jubilee*, 83.

7. Healthy Psychological Inventories, 28.

8. Jefferson, Thomas; Pay close attention to what your son, Solomon (I mean, Thomas Jefferson, had to say), 57; I started researching Thomas Jefferson, on the Internet, and in my home Encyclopedias, 66; "Am I the Reincarnation of Thomas Jefferson?" 66; Then, my family and I moved to Chicago, where I attended, first, Thomas Jefferson Elementary School, and lastly, DeVry University, 66; Thomas Jefferson is the reincarnation of Jacob, father of *the* renowned 12-boys that became known as Israel, 72; The sage(s) say that Prophet

Muhammad is the reincarnation of Moses. And Thomas Jefferson is the reincarnation of Jacob (the father of the 12 boys whose descendants became known as Israel), 88; Thomas Jefferson and the United States, 88.

9. Khalim; (the author) is the father of Noah, 21.

10. Lincoln, Abraham; As you know, Abraham Lincoln had a great impact on African Americans, 57; Your name, this time, will be Abraham Lincoln!58; After reading the selections that reference to Noah, read the selection, *Barack Obama to Complete the Presidency of Abraham Lincoln* (below) to learn more about how the USA fits into Bible Prophecy and about the discovery- revelation that President Barack Obama is the reincarnation of Abraham Lincoln, 61; On about June 21, 2008, I had a dream indicating that President Barack Obama is the reincarnation of Abraham Lincoln; I have watched Mr. Obama closely, and I am about 80% -100% certain that Barack Obama is the same soul as Abraham Lincoln, 66; After reading the selections that reference to Noah, read the selection, *Barack Obama to Complete the Presidency of Abraham Lincoln* (below) to learn more about how the USA fits into Bible Prophecy and about the discovery-revelation that President Barack Obama is the reincarnation of Abraham Lincoln, 66; President Barack Obama is the reincarnation of President Abraham Lincoln, 72; President Obama is finishing up his interrupted presidency as Abraham Lincoln, 73; Roboam, 1 Kings 11:43 Like Abraham Lincoln, 1861, 89; Abraham Lincoln saved the Union and is considered a moral Individual, 92.

11. MMPI; Observation #3 is of the father of the child, Noah, and it contains descriptions of the father using quotations from the MMPI, the Myers-Briggs Type Indicator, and the Brain Dominance theories, 3; The MMPI and Other Indices, 21; (An Example, Using Test Results From The MMPI), 28.

12. Moses; Who was Moses, Muhammad? 4; He will be taught that just like Moses, Aaron, Joshua, Malcolm, Martin, King David, King Solomon, the Pharaohs, the Hebrews, et.al., his

paternal roots are African. And he will be taught that he is one of the Sons of God, 14; Based on many verses in the Qur'an and the Bible, I had a suspicion that the Prophet Muhammad may be the reincarnation of Moses, "Is Prophet Muhammad the reincarnation of Moses?" I asked, 65; Mom and Dad let me "see" and "listen" to Moses, 71; Moses looked a lot like Isaac Hayes; Prophet Muhammad is the reincarnation of Moses. This *is* no joke, and it was presented to me as an almost obvious fact, 72; The sage(s) say that Prophet Muhammad is the reincarnation of Moses. And Thomas Jefferson is the reincarnation of Jacob (the father of the 12 boys whose descendants became known as Israel). The fact that Prophet Muhammad is the same soul as Moses creates an opportunity to psychologically, politically, religiously, and militarily disarm some terrorist elements, 88; *We are often reminded in the Qur'an that individuals are only responsible for their own deeds and thoughts. Why would Muhammad be guardian over the Torah and Gospel? The ...logical answer is that Muhammad (as Moses) helped reveal the Torah, and though not physically present, helped with the ministry of Jesus,* 88.

13. Muhammad; Who was Moses, Muhammad? 1; Based on many verses in the Qur'an and the Bible, I had a suspicion that the Prophet Muhammad may be the reincarnation of Moses, "Is Prophet Muhammad the reincarnation of Moses?" I asked, 65; Prophet Muhammad is the reincarnation of Moses, 72; The sage(s) say that Prophet Muhammad is the reincarnation of Moses. And Thomas Jefferson is the reincarnation of Jacob (the father of the 12 boys whose descendants became known as Israel). The fact that Prophet Muhammad is the same soul as Moses creates an opportunity to psychologically, politically, religiously, and militarily disarm some terrorist elements, 88; *Weare often reminded in the Qur'an that individuals are only responsible for their own deeds and thoughts. Why would Muhammad be guardian over the Torah and Gospel? The ...logical answer is that Muhammad (as Moses) helped*

*reveal theTorah, and though not physically present, helped with the ministry of Jesus,* 89.

14. Myers-Briggs Type Indicator, Observation #3 is of the father of the child, Noah, and it contains descriptions of the father using quotations from the MMPI, the Myers-Briggs Type Indicator, and the Brain Dominance theories, 3; 23;

15. Noah; Observation #3 is of the father of the child, Noah, 3; Observations of Noah, 7; (the author) is the father of Noah, 21; See "The Resurrection of Noah" for a fuller explanation, 23; Had dream about Noah on morning of 9/21/94, In the dream, Noah was about 3-4 years old, 37; Had dream about Noah on the morning of 10/9/94; In real life, Noah did get sick with a cold on Sunday night, Mon- day morning, about 2:30 A.M., according to Judy; 11-94. Had dream about Noah today, 38; (See *This World Is Mine* and *The Resurrection of Noah* for a fuller definition), 39; I am reminded of Jacob, Essau, Isaac, Rachel, Noah, etc., 53; Noah is now 18-years old. And it is over 17-years since I wrote the *Observations of Noah* on June 25,1995, 61; Noah is my delightful sun, 62; Noah is Great, 63; *Your Kingdom be strengthened* in Noah, 64; On 5/2/2000, I had the following experience during the period I was writing *The Resurrection of Noah*, 65; (See sunracommunications.com: *The Resurrection of Noah, The Second Coming*, et.al.), 74.

16. Obama, President Barack; After reading the selections that reference to Noah, read the selection, *Barack Obama to Complete the Presidency of Abraham Lincoln* (below) to learn more about how the USA fits into Bible Prophecy and about the discovery-revelation that President Barack Obama is the reincarnation of Abraham Lincoln, 61; *Your Kingdom be strengthened* in Noah, # In the earth, among your Chosen, In the 144, 000, In Barack and Michelle Obama, Sasha and Malia,*Tonya and Runako, # Chicagoland, And the United States of America *As it is in Heaven*, 64; On about June 21, 2008, I had a dream indicating that President Barack Obama is

the reincarnation of Abraham Lincoln; I have watched Mr. Obama closely, and I am about 80% - 100% certain that Barack Obama is the same soul as Abraham Lincoln, 66; *Barack Obama to Complete the Presidency of Abraham Lincoln,* 66; President Barack Obama is the reincarnation of President Abraham Lincoln, 72; President Obama is finishing up his interrupted presidency as Abraham Lincoln, 73; New Dispensation. Barack H. Obama, 2009, 91.

17. Payton, Walter, 22.

18. Susan; Susan (this is not her actual name), is the mother of Noah, 17.

19. The Second Coming; *The Second Coming of Christ* has already been described (set forth) by the prophets. And it is a great, massive learning that will take place, as the old systems fall, and new ones need to be ushered in for humanity to even survive on the earth plane; And, as these simultaneously occur throughout the network of those who have taken upon them- selves this leadership of the new age, there will be this Christ Consciousness of such a vibrational level that it may be deemed The Second Coming, or the Unity, 39; In the autobiography, *The Second Coming*, I tell you about what I saw, and what it means. I also tell, in some detail, about my quest, research, and experiences, The "Bibles" indicate that the Christian *"Second Coming"* started during the Clinton administration, 67; *The Second Coming* (this era) will change the political, military, economic, and social relationships of the USA - and the future of the world, 68; No wonder, *"Things Fall Apart."* (See sunracommunications.com: *The Resurrection of Noah, The Second Coming,* et.al.), 74.

20. Visions; What are visions? 4; Also, the materialist psychologists, and their fellow travelers don't understand dreams, visions, time, space, God, etc. And then a lot of them are liars and manipulators. A lot of them are busy trying to make a job for themselves, because of the irrational economic system that they live under. So, it is no wonder they have very limited success,

18; We believe that dreams and/or visions can be "normal" and useful. We believe in, and know something about "God," as should be the case with all normal human beings. *We believe in the dreams of Jacob, in the dreams of Joseph. We believe in the visions of Daniel, for instance; and we believe in the visions of John, the - Beloved.* From experience, I have a certain sense of the reliability of my own dreams or visions. And I also know that my own dreams and visions are in conformity with those of our ancestors- that I have just mentioned. And we know that our whole Judeo-Christian-Islamic tradition, and its real adherents believe essentially as I do. I also say that if the materialists were normal, they also would have dreams or visions, and they would better understand the nature of man. And since they are not normal, they must be dysfunctional, and abnormal. And since they don't know anything about God, and he's everywhere; again, the materialists must be abnormal. But I will tell you (if we can try to use an analogy), God is more like the weather. And you cannot stop summer, and you cannot stop winter- when it wants to come. You can only adjust to it, and you can study it. And even if you want to study the weather, you better have some respect. And you should realize that God is very much higher than the weather, 21; Introduction to Dreams and Visions, 26; "Visions" in healthy individuals are levels of experience sometime during the sleep state, but may be more possible when the mind and body have attained a certain amount of rest, or relaxation. Unlike dreams, where sometimes one knows that he is dreaming, in "visions," one is (then and there) conscious of the experience of the vision. Depending on the state of the individual, visions may contain high levels of energy. The subject matter of visions here, just like conscious experiences, cover a wide spectrum. They may involve objects, people, events, or places. And they may involve taking part in activities. When there is greater energy, there is usually greater clarity and/or understanding of what lesson(s) are to be learned. But, many experiences here, just like conscious experiences, have apparent limited usefulness. And like dreams, visions seem to only reflect past, or future "events." Visions seem to be a more direct interaction with what we would call spiritual forces, because, even though in a kind of sleep state, we are "conscious." And there is always the presence of moving energies. The prophets have generally described these as "winds," or seeming moving "flames," etc., 26; Finally, it should be noted that the author has practiced a variation of yoga, since 1971, and this has affected the quality (clarity) of his dreams, and/or visions, 27; Introduction to Dreams and Visions, 39.

21. Whole Brain Dominance; People should know whether they have left, right, or whole brain dominance, 1; The individual here possesses Whole Brain Dominance, 23; Then, I believe that "good," healthy, normal people, with normal, or above intelligence, with "whole brain dominance" (possibly, the "Mother of All Brains"), and "O Positive blood (possibly, the Mother of All Blood), and Unity within themselves can find better solutions to whatever problems we have because the DNA might be "better," 27.

# 22 ABOUT THE AUTHOR, AND OTHER BOOKS

Youssef Khalim obtained Unity in yoga on about 7/20/80. He says, "we will recombine into one faith, Judaism, Christianity, and Islam." He has been able to "see" and experience some amazing information about USA presidents Jefferson, Lincoln, and Obama; and also Prophets Moses, Muhammad, and Solomon - in visions, lucid dreams, and in meditation. Khalim makes reincarnation (resurrection) prominent again in our western religions. He resides in the Chicagoland area. And he is the father of Tonya, Runako, and Noah. His websites include:

http://sunracommunications.com

Other Books

Youssef Khalim's books include *People Of The Future/Day; You Are Too Beautiful; I Love You Back; You Look So Good; The Resurrection Of Noah; Jubilee Worldwide; Lara, Forever; Tanisha Love; Galina, All About Love; I Call My Sugar, Candie; Natalia, With Love; Svetlana, Angel Of Love; Lori, My Dream Girl*; *Love of My Life*; and *The Second Coming!*

www.ingramcontent.com/pod-product-compliance
Lightning Source LLC
Chambersburg PA
CBHW032049090426
42744CB00004B/144